OUR STORY...
His STORY

One couple's encounter with the Grace of God
in the Crucible of Affliction

RICK ROOD

PRESS

Our Story...His Story
One couple's encounter with the Grace of God in the Crucible of Affliction
by Rick Rood

Printed in the United States of America
Edited by Xulon Press

ISBN 9781498420846

Some of the material incorporated into this book has appeared in the following published articles. The author expresses his gratitude for the permission to use this material granted by each of the listed publications and ministries.

The following articles appeared in the magazine Chera Fellowship, a quarterly publication of IFCA International, for those who have lost a mate: "Fingerprints" (Summer 2007), "How God Produces Love" (Summer 2008), "Who Am I, Anyway?" (Summer 2009), "Letting Go, and Moving On" (Spring 2010).

The following articles appeared in the magazine Challenger, a quarterly publication of the Chinese Christian Mission: "Caring for Polly—Long Term with Love" (April-June 2009), "Doubt and Faith" (Jan-Mar 2010), "The Lord Our Shepherd" (Oct-Dec 2010), "How to Help the Suffering" (Oct-Dec 2012).

The following article appeared in the periodical Dallas Connection, the alumni publication of Dallas Theological Seminary: "A Husband's Journey" (Fall 2006).

The following articles are posted on the website of Probe Ministries (www.probe.org): "Reflections of a Caregiver," "Grief and Grace," and "The Truth About Heaven."

www.xulonpress.com

DEDICATION

This book is dedicated to all those who suffer affliction in this life, and to those who care for them. Most of all, however, it is dedicated to the Lord Jesus Christ, without whose mercy and grace our story would never have become His story.

TABLE OF CONTENTS

Dedication . . . . *iii*
Acknowledgements . . . . *vii*
Endorsements . . . . *ix*
Introduction . . . . *xi*

Part 1: Early Years–God's Preparing Grace

Chapter I:	*Polly*	*17*
Chapter II:	*Marriage and Beyond*	*24*
Chapter III:	*Freshman Pastor*	*34*
Chapter IV:	*Back to Dallas—1981*	*45*

Part 2: Twenty Years in the Crucible–God's Preserving Grace

Chapter V:	*The Life We Didn't Want*	*53*
Chapter VI:	*A New Beginning*	*64*
Chapter VII:	*A New Home for Polly...and for Me*	*77*
Chapter VIII:	*Helping the Suffering*	*91*
Chapter IX:	*The God of All Comfort*	*105*
Chapter X:	*The Lord, Our Shepherd*	*114*
Chapter XI:	*Increasing Challenges*	*126*
Chapter XII:	*A Long Obedience[1]*	*142*
Chapter XIII:	*Should a Christian Use a Physician?*	*154*
Chapter XIV:	*Final Days*	*160*

Part 3: Aftermath–Some Perspectives on God's Grace

Chapter XV: *Reflections—God's Transforming Grace* . . *173*

Chapter XVI: *When Life Seems Unfair—God's*
                  Sustaining Grace *185*

Chapter XVII: *Letting Go and Moving On—God's*
                  Comforting Grace *202*

Chapter XVIII: The Hope of Glory—God's Future Grace[2] . *216*

Some Closing Words *231*

About the Author *237*

Endnotes *239*

ACKNOWLEDGEMENTS

————

This book would never have been written were it not for the many friends who have urged me for several years to put our story in print. Dr. Wesley Willmer was the first person who suggested this project. I also want to thank my brother Paul Rood, my sister-in-law Dr. Judith Mendelsohn Rood, my friends Dr. Mark Talbot of Wheaton College and Dr. Scott Horrell of Dallas Theological Seminary who read the manuscript and made several helpful suggestions. I want to thank Dr. Horrell for the many hours of conversation and prayer (usually in the early hours of the morning over breakfast) in reflecting on the Lord's grace in our life.

I cannot be thankful enough for my parents, Don and Bea Rood (both now in heaven), for being used by God to point me to our Savior. I miss them both. I thank God as well for Pastors Ray Stedman and David Roper whose faithful teaching of God's

Word helped to nurture my walk with the Lord as a young person at Peninsula Bible Church in Palo Alto, CA.

I thank my dear wife Polly who endured so many years of hardship. I will never forget her example of patient and even joyful endurance. I also thank my precious new wife Li Lin for her unselfish encouragement in bringing this book to completion.

I particularly thank Polly's family who even though they lived at a distance for most of our married life, they expressed their love to us. They suffered the loss of their daughter and sister as only a family member can fully understand.

What flaws remain in this book are purely my own. My prayer, however, is that the Lord's mercies will shine through its pages, to his glory, and to the blessing and encouragement of those who read it.

ENDORSEMENTS

"Nothing penetrates our lives with the grace of our Lord as the experiences of our friends. And nothing reveals the kindness of God more wondrously than suffering. Since their single days in college, Rick and Polly have been good friends. Through Polly's long illness and death, Rick shares extraordinary insights of the 'severe mercy' that renews our trust in the living God."

~ Scott Horrell, PhD. Professor of Theological Studies, Dallas Theological Seminary

"I'm thankful that the Lord has enabled my dear brother-in-law to write this book. I know that it will bless others who are struggling to understand, support, encourage, and help loved ones suffering from long term illness, or any other life altering condition. I witnessed Rick and Polly's journey together for twenty years. I was touched by what I saw as the Lord instilled in them a faith, courage and love that carried them through this experience, one day at a time. Those years were never easy, yet I saw the Lord work in their lives in very concrete ways. I know that this memoir will be a blessing to the families and friends of those who are on a similar journey. Please read it and share it with others!"

~ Judith Mendelsohn Rood, PhD. Professor of History and Middle Eastern Studies, Biola University

"*Our Story...His Story* shows how God graciously wills to strengthen his people to be faithful to each other and to Him in the midst of long-lasting affliction."

~ Mark R. Talbot, PhD. Associate Professor of Philosophy, Wheaton College

"I knew Rick and Polly before they were married. And I followed their lives particularly over the long course of Polly's illness. Theirs is a story of struggle and perseverance. Most of all, however, it is a story of God's upholding grace in the face of human weakness. I pray God will use this book to encourage many others who are navigating the unavoidable storms of life."

~ Wesley K. Willmer, PhD. Former Vice-President for Advancement, Biola University

INTRODUCTION

(To Be Read)

―――⊸⊸⊸⊸――

"The fact of suffering undoubtedly constitutes the single greatest challenge to Christian faith."[3] These were the words of the late John Stott. This is no doubt true, not only for the skeptic, but also for the believer. For the skeptic, suffering poses a *barrier* to faith. "How can belief in a good and powerful God be reconciled with a world of evil and pain?" For the believer, however, it poses a *test* of faith. Suffering tests our faith in the goodness and power of the One to whom we have entrusted our very lives. "If God loves me, why has He allowed me to suffer in the ways I have?"

This book is the simple story of our life. It's a story of persevering hope, of fragile faith and love. Most of all, however, it is a story of God's preserving grace in the crucible of affliction.

When someone decides to tell their story, some natural reservations come to mind. For one, everyone has a story—and some people's stories are more worthy of being told than ours. Then, in telling one's story, there's always the temptation to focus just on ourselves and how much we have been through, or how much faith our life has required of us. Yet there is also the recognition that if God can use our story to encourage and help others who are also facing a dark season of life, then our story is worth being told.

All of us would like to believe that if we belong to God, and if we are faithful to Him the best we can be, we should be spared the afflictions that plague our race—or at least the really serious ones. There are some who seem to preach just such a message.

There are indeed times when God wonderfully delivers us from our troubles; and who knows how many troubles God has spared us from even being exposed to? However, there are also times when He allows the troubles to remain and mercifully carries us through them. The eleventh chapter of the Letter to the Hebrews recounts the experience of many who by faith *conquered kingdoms, performed acts of righteousness, obtained promises, shut the mouths of lions, quenched the power of fire, escaped the edge of the sword, from weakness were made strong, became mighty in war, put foreign armies to flight....* Yet it also records the experience of those who endured *mockings and scourgings, yes also chains and imprisonment...who were stoned, sawn in two...tempted...put to death with the sword and who went about in sheepskins, in goatskins, being destitute, afflicted, ill-treated (men of whom the world was not worthy), wandering in deserts and mountains and caves and holes in the ground* (Hebrews 11:33-38). It wasn't for a lack of faith that the latter group experienced such trials. In fact, they are included in this list because of their faith. It was on account of their faith in God that they were able to endure such afflictions. It's in the crucible of affliction that our faith is tested, but it's also in the crucible of affliction that God's faithfulness is proven.

When we see God's miraculous interventions, it's not difficult to trust Him. Yet our faith is tested and refined when we don't see and we don't understand what He is doing in our lives. Perhaps this is one reason why Jesus said to Thomas, *Blessed are they who did not see, and yet believed* (John 20:29). There is a tendency for us to exalt a faith that lifts us out of and above the storms of life. It's the biblical view, however, that a faith that enables us to endure life's stormy seasons is of like precious value.

I've written our story from my own personal vantage point. For reasons that may become clear as the story unfolds, it would be impossible for me to tell it fully or accurately from my wife Polly's perspective. For this reason it may at times be difficult to fully hear her voice. Yet I hope you will hear enough to gain a glimpse of the kind of person she was.

My purpose in writing is not to paint a portrait of ourselves as anything other than what we were: two ordinary people, struggling with the same frailties, fears, sins and doubts as anyone else. My hope and prayer, however, is that by listening to our story your trust in our gracious and merciful, yet mysterious God will be strengthened, that you might find hope both for this life and the next—for our story is really His story.

Part 1

EARLY YEARS:
GOD'S PREPARING GRACE

Chapter I

POLLY

O f all the times for my pager to go off, this seemed like the least convenient occasion. A young man who had spent several weeks in the ICU in the hospital where I served as chaplain had recently died; and I was sitting in the sanctuary of a nearby church as the pastor conducted his funeral.

I had learned, however, that rarely did anyone page me if the reason was not important or urgent. So I slipped out to call the number that appeared on my pager. I recognized it as the number of the nursing home where my wife Polly resided. "Hello, Rick. This is Polly's nurse. She's having serious breathing problems and we're sending her across the street to Lake Pointe Hospital. You need to meet her there in the ER as soon as you can." For the past nineteen years, Polly had experienced the slow decline that accompanies Huntington's Disease,[4] a neurodegenerative illness. For nearly nine years I had cared for her at home, but for the past eleven years the nursing home had been her residence, having entered when she was just 41 years of age. It had become my "second home" as well. This was not the first time during these years that she had been hospitalized—usually for pneumonia. She had seemed fine, however, when I saw her the previous evening. I walked out to the parking lot and got in my car and started off on the twenty minute drive to the hospital.

As I maneuvered the familiar route, I thought about the unusual occurrence of the day before—but more about that later. I also thought back over our nearly 32 years of marriage. It all began back in 1970 when we were both students at Seattle Pacific University (Seattle Pacific College back then). We had met briefly on one or two occasions during the first couple years of college. We became better acquainted, however, when we both ran for student body office the end of our sophomore year—Polly for secretary (unopposed); and I for 1st Vice President (a position that would give me responsibility for planning and conducting our monthly student chapels).

During our "campaign" for office I had taken note of Polly. We were not at all the same. I had grown up in what would later come to be known as "Silicon Valley" in California. She was a "country" girl, growing up in the Willamette Valley of central Oregon. When Polly would tell her roommate that she was going to take the bus from the urban college campus to the downtown district of Seattle, she would say, "I'm going into town." Her roommate would point out, "Polly, you *are* in town." She obviously couldn't quite shake her rural sense of geography.

There was something special about Polly. She was about 5'4", had brown hair, brown eyes and faintly visible freckles. When I walked into the student body office she often greeted me with her contagious smile and a twinkle in her eye. She was cheerful and eager to serve. Most importantly, she had an evident faith in and love for the Lord. She had spent the summer prior to serving in student government as part of a mission team in British Columbia, putting on camps for the children of local Native American families. In fact, she had spent the two summers prior to that working at Christian camps in Oregon and Washington.

Polly was a multi-faceted girl. Her family told me that she loved to read. She especially enjoyed reading science fiction for some reason. She devoured C. S. Lewis' "Space Trilogy" and J. R. R. Tolkien's "The Hobbit." She also had competed on her school's swim team, as well as being selected for her high school cheer leading squad.

When I visited her home in Oregon, she loved to drive with me up to nearby Mary's Peak, the tallest mount in the Pacific Coastal Range. From the summit we could look east and see across the valley to the Cascade Mountains in the far distance. We also loved to drive an hour or so to Newport, a delightful town on the coast, where we could walk the beautiful beaches.

Polly had also learned to play piano quite well, and even the guitar. In fact, she had chosen Seattle Pacific because they were known to have a strong music program. Polly told me that she had hoped to major in music. She was humble enough, however, to tell me that her professor had informed her that she likely would not have excelled in that field. So she decided to major in elementary education, with a minor in history.

I will never forget seeing Polly one evening kneeling at a chair in the student government office next to a fellow classmate, in prayer. That told me something about her that nothing else quite could.

As the school year wore on, and we worked together in the office week after week, we slowly grew attached to one another. There was something in me that wanted to guard her and protect her. I believe she realized that. One evening as we were talking, she said to me, "Rick, you might as well know now. There's a fifty percent chance that I might someday have Huntington's Disease. This is the illness my father died from a couple years ago—and I might have it someday too." I respected her for telling me this. I don't remember what I said. I had never met anyone with Huntington's Disease (HD). I had never even heard of it before.

The next day, when I looked up a description of HD in a textbook in the college library, I was quite sobered. As are most neurodegenerative illnesses, HD is a serious and debilitating disease. Most people with the illness survive anywhere from ten to twenty years after onset. Children of those who carry the genetic trait for this illness have a fifty percent chance of having it—but also a fifty percent chance of *not* having it. Onset of the illness may come during childhood or adolescence for some. For most, however, it comes later on in life. At that time, there was no test to determine if one carried this trait or not. One just waited to see.

As Polly had told me, her father had recently died with HD. Until she represented her family at his funeral in Oklahoma City, she had not seen him in many years. Her parents had gone their separate ways when Polly was about eight years old, and she had not seen him all these years.

Polly had been sheltered from knowing exactly what her father had, until she was in her junior year in high school. When she did learn of her father's condition, her mom said to her, "Polly, this can either make you or break you." Polly's mother Elsie was a gifted and respected school teacher, and a very strong woman. She had a firm faith in the Lord and she loved her three children (two daughters and a son) very much. I would later come to understand something of what she carried in her heart for her children all those many years.

In spite of this unexpected news, I found my love for Polly growing. Yet I was troubled about the prospect of her having HD someday. I decided to seek out some counsel from the people I most respected. I talked with my own mother one day about Polly and this news she had shared with me. I remember Mom (also a school teacher and principal, as well as a gifted musician) saying to me, "Rick, none of us knows what we might have in life." When she met Polly for the first time later that year, she said to me, "Polly really is for you."

I decided to also seek out the counsel of my pastor, whom I had grown to greatly respect as a warm hearted and insightful Bible teacher. He knew and loved both of us and he was more than encouraging with regard to the development of our relationship.

About that time we learned that Polly's younger brother Chris was beginning to show signs of the illness. I believe he was only about fourteen years of age. Chris was a sweet young boy. He had his sister's smile and contagious laughter. When I went to visit Polly at her home in Philomath, Oregon, Chris loved to shoot baskets with me out front of their house.

Seeing what was beginning to happen to Chris prompted me to do more research on the illness; and one article I read I interpreted as suggesting that when it's the father who passes on the trait, affected children may have a tendency to come down with the illness earlier in life. This is what was happening with Chris. I think the fact that it was not happening to Polly gave us hopes that she had escaped it—and so we hoped and prayed that she had.

Chapter II

MARRIAGE AND BEYOND

—◁◁◁◁ᘓᘓᘓᘓ▷▷▷—

The decision to get married is not an easy decision for anyone. The Apostle Paul tells us that though marriage is a divinely inspired relationship, there are certain advantages to remaining unmarried (I Cor. 7). Our Lord Himself said that there are some whom God calls to the single life (Mt. 19:11-13). Nevertheless, marriage does seem to be God's design for most.

Neither is the decision *whom* to marry an easy one to make. While in the midst of a "dating" relationship we try to see clearly through the fog of our emotions to gain a true glimpse of the heart and character of the person we are getting to know. None of us, however, is omniscient. None of us can fully know what lies in another person's heart, or even in our own. Nor can we know what the future might hold for the two of us should we commit our lives to one another. A friend of mine once told me, "Rick, every relationship is a journey of faith."[5] I believe he was right. When we make commitments that will impact the rest of our lives, we do so deliberately and prayerfully, based on what evidence God enables us to see. Eventually, though, we must make a decision based on what we know, either to commit or not. In the end, however, we must trust God for what we cannot see, even about the person we are marrying.

Our wedding was a wonderful event. Polly and her family were well known in the surrounding area. Some of our friends from college in Seattle, as well as many of my family's friends from California descended on the quiet little village of Blodget, Oregon. I'm sure there have been many weddings in that little country church—but probably none quite like this one. The church was packed to overflowing, as my dear father, assisted by Polly's pastor Jerry Kennedy, conducted the wedding, September 11, 1971.

Polly had prayed for a sunny day and God gave us exactly what she prayed for. I must say that she looked more beautiful as a bride than I had even expected. As she took my arm, I could sense the tremor in her hand. Before long, however, her nerves and hand were calmed.

Marriage prompted us to consider seriously God's direction for our life. Early in my college experience I had felt God's leading toward ministry—not simply because my father was a minister, but mostly because the study and teaching of God's Word during the years our family spent at Peninsula Bible Church in Palo Alto, California, had impacted my life more than anything. I remember my pastor from my high school years saying to me once, "Rick, I think you have the heart for ministry. I hope you consider going to seminary." Even as a young person I felt there was no better way to invest my life than to somehow minister the Word of God to others. In time, the Lord seemed to confirm that this was his purpose for my life, giving me opportunity to teach the Bible in the college ministry at my church in the Seattle area. Polly likewise had a hunger for God's Word, and a desire to be used by Him. We looked forward to serving the Lord together in some way.

During those days the Lord also opened doors to learn to share the Christian message with others whom He brought across our path. One such experience occurred as I was eating lunch one day in the student union on campus at Seattle Pacific. I noticed a student sitting alone nearby, so I introduced myself. He told me he was new to the school—a transfer student. I asked him how things were going for him. "Fine" he said. "But you know," he continued, "I've been taking one of these required Bible courses. Some of the students in the class keep talking about a 'personal relationship' with Jesus Christ. I'm not sure I know what they're talking about."

Well, I almost swallowed my sandwich whole. For the next several minutes I did my best to explain to him what the Bible tells us about how to know Christ. I shared with him how God made us and desires a relationship with us, but that we had rebelled against Him, and turned away from his will for us. Consequently, our relationship with God is broken. This is the ultimate cause of all the troubles in our world, and of death itself. I shared with him how the Bible teaches that there is nothing we can do to remedy our situation and mend our relationship with God, but that He had taken the initiative in sending his Son, Jesus Christ, into the world to make payment for our sin, in our place. He did this through his death on the cross. It's as we acknowledge our sin against God, and turn to Him by placing our faith and trust in Christ, that we can be forgiven, and our relationship with God can be mended, both for this life and for eternity. Just as we might trust in a doctor to provide what we need to overcome a physical illness, or in a lawyer to represent us in a court of law to resolve a legal claim against us, so we must place our trust in Christ to restore our broken relationship with God, made possible by his death in our place.[6]

When I asked him if this is something he wanted to do, he said, "Yes, it really is." I will never forget bowing with him in that crowded student union, as he entrusted his life to Christ. A few days later we met there again, and he told me that he had gone home and shared what I had told him with his wife. She too had trusted in Christ. The Lord brought other people into their life throughout that school year, but we had enough contact with them to see them grow in their relationship with the Lord.

After graduation from college, Polly and I prepared to leave the Pacific Northwest for Dallas, Texas where I would attend Dallas Theological Seminary (DTS). Packing up all our earthly belongings in our little Toyota Corolla, and a small U-Haul trailer, we headed south. We would miss much about the Northwest, including our many friends.

Moving from the wet climate and green and mountainous terrain of the Puget Sound area of Washington State to the flat and dry plains of north Texas in early August of 1972 was a shock to say the least. We had never experienced such scorching heat, nor seen so many bugs in all our life. Not only that, but at that time, before the oil crisis that would strike a couple years later, we had never before seen so many luxury cars being driven as we did in Dallas. We were truly in the land of Lincolns and Cadillacs.

The people of Dallas we found to be among the friendliest we had ever met. I think nearly every cashier at every store we shopped at back then bid us farewell with the same phrase, "Y'all come back now, ya hear?" When a funeral procession came down the roadway, all the drivers pulled over to the side of the road to pay their quiet respects.

Seminary life proved to be an immense challenge, especially at first. DTS is known for its rigorous curriculum. Though this is a good thing, the unwary freshman student, especially one newly married, can find that the demands of seminary studies can undermine the health of his marriage and of his personal spiritual life. It's a shame that a course of study that is intended to prepare men and women for a lifetime of spiritual ministry can, if not approached with prudence, actually work against the spiritual health of its students. It's not the fault of the school. There is no committee of faculty members sitting down to plot the spiritual destruction of their students. Much to the contrary. Yet it takes a great deal of wisdom for a young person to work just as hard to strengthen his relationships with his spouse and with his Lord, as he does in fulfilling the requirements of the curriculum. The Master of Theology program at Dallas is a four year program. Some of my classmates stretched it out to five years. This seems like a long time to devote to seminary, but in my estimation, it is a wise option for many students.

One of the things God did during our seminary years was to teach us something about his ability to provide for us—something we would desperately need to know in years to come. Shortly before departing for Dallas I had been informed that a foundation in California was intending to cover the cost of my tuition at DTS. We just needed to work to provide for our living, which we did. I don't know why He provided for us in this way, while so many of my classmates had to struggle harder to balance work and studies. God apparently knew that considering our make-up, and what we would face later in life, this was the only way we would make it through.

We also learned that a former teaching colleague of my mother's had moved from California to Dallas to take a job as principal at a Christian school. He graciously gave Polly a job as teacher's aide our first year in Dallas. Another job at an insurance company in downtown Dallas opened up for Polly our remaining years there. Though there were the normal stresses of being married to a seminary student, she was so willing to support me in following what we believed was God's leading in our life. I also worked cleaning swimming pools part time during our seminary years.

Seminary life wasn't all work though. We even took time for tennis lessons. Most significantly, however, we forged some wonderful friendships during those years. We used to meet once a month with four other couples, for dinner and a fun evening together. Though we all have scattered in different directions since then, we have remained friends through the years.

Of course, as with many seminary students at that time, we lived virtually from paycheck to paycheck. We were on what then was called a "pop bottle budget." Our budget was so lean that we knew how many pop bottles we had on hand, which at that time could be turned in at various outlets for a dime or so per bottle. A couple of six packs of empty bottles could come close to buying a hamburger. One day I recall being broke at the end of the month, and needing some cash for something related to my being in a friend's wedding. This was an unusual circumstance. I can't remember what it was, but I remember that it cost $11.25. I was worried as to what I would do. I don't think I even had a credit card (thankfully). To my surprise, that day I received a check in the mail from a friend across the country, in the amount of $11.25. Not $10.00 or even $11.00, but $11.25. I chocked it up as an "unusual coincidence."

As we neared graduation, we were praying about what the Lord wanted for us next. We had hoped that perhaps God might lead us to return to Seattle and work in some aspect of pastoral ministry, but we didn't have any indication that He was opening the door for this to become a reality. One day during my senior year, I met near the campus for lunch with Dr. Bill Lawrence. I had known Bill from the years living in the Bay Area. He had served as a summer intern at my home church in Palo Alto, and had later taken up pastoring what became a thriving church in San Jose. When he came to Dallas from time to time on ministry trips, I would try to see him. On this occasion he told me that two couples from his church in San Jose had recently moved to the Seattle area and were interested in forming a new church. He wondered if I might be interested in serving as their pastor. Of course I was.

Even though the prospect of assuming the responsibility of pastoring was intimidating (I was only 26), I felt that this was God's direction for us—and Polly bravely followed.

The night before we left Dallas for the west coast, while we were loading up our rental truck, Polly tripped on the stairs leading up to our apartment. A visit to the local ER revealed she had fractured her ankle. We left the next morning for the Bay Area, where we spent the summer interning at my home church in Palo Alto— her leg, snuggly casted, resting on the front seat of the truck.

When we left Dallas in June of 1976, we had come to love this city and its people. I will be forever grateful for what God did for us during those years, and for the foundation for a lifetime of ministry that I received at DTS. We were now beginning a new chapter in life's journey.

Chapter III

FRESHMAN PASTOR

When the group of three couples invited us to come to Seattle to help them in starting a new church, they had never even heard me preach. It's probably a good thing. If they had, they may not have called us. I'm sure that this group thought more than twice during those early months about whether to keep me on, but for some reason they did. Oh, thank God for his tender mercies and the patience of his people.

Over the course of those first nine months, we met as a home Bible study; and I supplemented the small income they provided for us by teaching at a church based Bible school in the area. This was almost enough to meet our needs, but not quite. One day, as I was standing in the office of this Bible school, the secretary received a phone call from a church in a town on the Olympic Peninsula, asking if she knew of anyone who might want to come once a week and teach at a Bible school they were starting. She looked at me and asked, "Are you interested in teaching at another Bible school over in Sequim?" I certainly was. The additional income just helped meet our monthly budget.

The first Christmas we resided in the Seattle area we decided to fly to San Francisco to spend a few days with my family who lived at that time in Sunnyvale, just down the peninsula. We actually left on Christmas Eve, one of the busiest days of the year for travelers. When we arrived in San Francisco, we slowly made our way across the crowded terminal toward the exit. Suddenly, someone pressed in on us from behind. We turned to look. We could hardly believe our eyes. It was the couple who had come to know the Lord five years previously in Seattle! We had sadly lost contact with them—but what a delight to see them. "Where are you going?" we asked. "Well, we're headed for the Philippines, as missionary school teachers." We could hardly believe our ears. We hugged and parted ways. I believe the Lord wanted us to know what He had been doing in the life of this young couple. Hardly a "mere coincidence."

Over the next several months our home Bible study group started attracting others who were interested in studying God's Word. Then in April of 1977, we met for the first time as an established church body, Forestview Community Church, renting space at the Seventh Day Adventist Church in Edmonds, Washington.

The motto of Dallas Seminary is "Preach the Word." It appears in Greek on the school insignia: *Keruxon ton Logon*. If there was one thing I knew to do as a young pastor, it was to do exactly that. Over the next four years, I had the opportunity of preaching through Paul's Epistle to the Romans, the Gospel of Luke, Hebrews, the Upper Room Discourse in John's Gospel, Ephesians, Philippians, and several other biblical passages. There is no greater privilege than being one of God's messengers to a body of believers. There are few greater blessings for a young pastor than having a congregation of very patient listeners.

One thing I learned very quickly, however, was that there was a lot about pastoring that I had learned little about in seminary. How to deal with a group of people with diverse ideas about how a church should go. How to carry out the many pastoral duties that come with the position: conducting weddings and funerals, baptizing new believers, counseling people with a myriad of issues, some of which I had never even thought of.

In those early years, God brought some wonderful people to our small congregation. One of them was Bill and Dorothea Hart, parents of one of our Elders, Bill Hart, Jr. Bill Sr. had contracted Parkinson's Disease early in their married life, and Dorothea had devoted herself to caring for her husband, which she did with amazing grace. They became regular attenders at our church. I can still see them now, Bill slowly shuffling along with Dorothea patiently at his side, finding their way to near the front of our little congregation of about 100 or less, and patiently listening to the sermons of this fledgling pastor. From time to time I would receive hand written notes from Dorothea, thanking me for one of my messages, and telling me she was praying for me. This godly woman did more to encourage me than she could ever know.

The greatest of all blessings, during our years serving this church, was the birth of our two children. During the early years of our marriage, we had prayed about whether we should have a family. Having a family is not an easy decision for any couple. No one knows what the future might hold—for their children, or for themselves. This is especially true, however, for couples who are in the position we were in. No parent would intentionally lay on their children the burden of Huntington's Disease. No one would want someone to have this illness. Yet it's normal for couples to want to have a family; and no one believes this will happen to them. Years before, we had asked Polly's former pastor to join us in a day of prayer and fasting with regard to this very matter. During the seminary years I had also sought the counsel of one of my profs, and he had been very encouraging. We did not know if Polly would ever have Huntington's Disease (HD). In fact, we had reason to hope that she might not.

Though since the mid-1990s there has been a test to see if a person carries the HD trait, only a small percentage are choosing to be tested. Even the woman whose research contributed to the ultimate development of the genetic test for HD (and who is at risk for the illness herself) has declined to take it.[7] Though this may seem difficult for others to comprehend, it is understandable that most people choose to live with a sense of hopefulness about their future. There's something in the human heart that cries out for hope. My one word of advice to others is to prayerfully seek God's wisdom—and seek the prayerful counsel of godly friends.[8]

Based on what information we had about Polly at the time, on the encouragement we received from others, and on our innate sense of God's goodness, we decided to begin a family. Our dear son was born just one week before our church officially began meeting. What a week that was, giving birth to our firstborn child, as well as to our church. He was "all boy" from the very beginning. He even surprised his nurses in the hospital, when on his third day after birth, he actually raised himself up on his arms, essentially performing a "push up." They could hardly believe it.

Three years later, our precious daughter was born. Her temperament was much different than her brother's. When we brought her home from the hospital, her brother looked at her in her crib, and said in a rather disappointed tone, "She doesn't talk, does she." He quickly turned to resume his play in our back yard. I can truly say that there has been no greater blessing in life, from a human perspective, than bringing our two children into the world. Though out of respect for their privacy I've chosen to mention them only briefly in this book, we love them dearly, and would not trade them for anything.

When Polly was in the hospital for the birth of our son one of the doctors approached me. He was the anesthesiologist assigned to Polly's care. He asked me, "Are you related to Dr. Paul Rood?" I said, "Yes. He was my grandfather." My grandfather had been pastor of First Covenant Church in Seattle back in the 1920s. For a few years in the 1930s he was also President of the Bible Institute of Los Angeles (now Biola University). As a pastor and evangelist, God used him to touch the lives of countless people. This doctor had known him, or at least known of him. He said to me, "I'd like to donate my services without charge for your baby's birth." We were very grateful. Three years later, he did the same when our daughter was born. I believe we really needed this encouragement regarding the birth of our dear children.

Not all of our experiences during those years, however, were quite so pleasant and encouraging. Adultery, divorce, rebellious teenagers, and addictions were occasional matters of attention. One young man in our congregation had even experienced threats from the Mafia. One Sunday, at the end of our service, a man came marching down the aisle of the church waving a gun in his hand. He pulled me into a side room and told me that he would have someone seriously harmed if he didn't apologize for having an affair with his wife.

Every young pastor enters ministry with a strong dose of idealism; and this is good. It's our idealism that prompts us to dream, and to attempt great things for the Lord. Nevertheless, idealism can lead to unrealistic expectations, which can lead to disillusionment when they are not met (and they won't be). I'm convinced that the first five years of ministry are designed to temper our idealism with a large dose of reality—about ourselves and about the ministry. Whether we pass this test will have a lot to do with our ability to remain in ministry for the long haul.

In time, I found myself longing to return to the seminary for further studies in theology. One of the things I had learned about myself in the pastorate was that I had a bent toward teaching, and an inquiring mind that would not stop. After a few years pastoring, I eventually took steps to investigate the possibility of entering the PhD program back at DTS. Much to my surprise, I received a letter of acceptance, contingent on the approval of my examining committee at the seminary. I made arrangements to fly to Dallas for a few days to meet with the committee, and to investigate any opportunities for work and ministry in Dallas, should we return. Polly agreed to pray with me about this proposed change.

After receiving the approval of my examining committee for entrance into the doctoral program, I went across campus to talk with my friend Bob Salstrom, who was the Alumni Director at that time. I told him of our plans, and asked him if he knew of any ministry openings in the area. He thought for a moment, and then said, "You know, there's a fellow who just resigned his position here at the seminary last Friday. Why don't you go down the hall and talk with Dr. Constable about taking his position in the Field Education Dept.?" I did just that.

Dr. Constable and I spoke for maybe ten minutes. I left later that day to return home to Seattle. This was on a Monday. A few days later Dr. Constable called me and asked if I wanted the position. I accepted his offer.

Well, the wheels were set in motion. I looked at Polly and said, "We're going to have to sell our house." We called a friend who was a realtor and told him of our plans. He came over that evening and drew up the papers necessary for us to put our house on the market. We had no idea how long this might take.

The very next morning, he brought a young couple to our home. They loved the house and they agreed to buy it at our asking price. We were amazed. Several weeks later, when we informed our church leaders of our plans, they said, "You're going to have a hard time selling your house." I said, "Well, it's already sold." They were amazed.

Of course, our decision to return to Dallas put our church elders in the position of having to search for a new pastor. I'm not sure they were relishing this idea. Conducting a pastoral search can be a very intense and difficult process. A few weeks after we had made the decision to return to Dallas, however, a friend of mine from my youth, Conrad Hopkins, came by our home for a visit. He had just finished studies at Regent College in Vancouver, B.C., and he was looking for a church to pastor. I said to him, "You just may have come to the right place, at the right time." Eventually, the church ended up calling Conrad as their pastor and he had a very effective ministry there for several years.

During these years of pastoring, Polly served very faithfully as wife, mother and friend to many in the church. She was not an "up front" kind of person, but she had a loving heart and a warm and humble presence—and she showed it in small ways. She loved to bake. Every Christmas she baked special loaves of bread for all the elders' families in our church. Her primary ministry, however, was encouraging me and keeping our home a welcoming refuge.

Many churches have unrealistic expectations of a pastor's wife. They expect her to teach Bible studies or lead a women's ministry. Indeed, some are gifted in these ways and find time to serve in visible ways in the church. Our church was wise, however, in letting Polly know that her primary ministry was to me. That's the kind of ministry she fulfilled. Perhaps she was too encouraging to me at times. Some likely hoped that she would offer more frequent and insightful critiques of my sermons, but this was not Polly's gift. She was an encourager—and I'm thankful she was.

The church gave us a wonderfully gracious send-off, sharing many memories of the previous five years. Now, however, Polly and I and our two young children were heading back to Dallas to begin yet another chapter in our lives.

Chapter IV

BACK TO DALLAS – 1981

Returning to Dallas after five years away was like returning "home." This time, though, I was returning not as a student but as a young faculty member. Actually, I think I was the youngest member of the faculty at that time. I felt very much out of place sitting in faculty meetings with men whom I had studied under just five years previously. Understandably, I wondered what I possibly had to offer the students.

However, God had made a niche for me there. I was close enough in age to the students that I could still identify with their needs and struggles. Yet the Lord had also given me enough experience in pastoring to pass on something meaningful to them. In addition to overseeing the pastoral internships, one of my assignments was to teach a course called "Praxis of Pastoral Ministry." This class provided instruction in how to conduct weddings, funerals, communion, baptism and a host of other things that young pastors find themselves doing. I knew all too well how much the students needed this course. In addition, I was able to pursue doctoral studies in theology, with the hope of one day teaching in this field.

When we had first moved back to Dallas, we were a bit concerned about finding a place to live. At first, considering my beginning salary at the seminary, our realtor told us that we might have a hard time finding a good place to live. A couple days later, however, a graduating DTS student walked into the realtor's office wanting to sell his home. She called us and said, "This house will be very suitable for you and within your ability to finance." We were very thankful.

A few years later we were able to afford a bit larger home just a mile away. One of the welcome blessings was discovering that the couple who lived directly across the street was a missionary couple who had served with Central America Mission (now Camino Global), Al and Jeane Olson. Al, however, had contracted an unusual neurodegenerative illness early in life and he and Jeane had to return to the states, where she could work in the home office of the mission. They became not only our neighbors, but our dear friends. It would not be too long before I understood why the Lord had planted us directly across the street from Al and Jeane, just as He had guided Bill and Dorothea Hart to our congregation in Seattle years earlier. We had experienced enough "coincidences" in life by this point to know that such experiences were anything but that. I believe that in his providence God had planned that we should be exposed to the wonderful example and love of these two dear couples.

During the summer of 1983, we decided it would be good for Polly to spend a week or so with her mother, step-father and family back in Oregon—just for a brief vacation with her loved ones. She enjoyed her time very much. At the end of the summer, we joined her parents at Polly's grandmother's home in the little town of DeQueen, Arkansas, for a family reunion. These were always enjoyable times. During our stay there, however, Polly's step-father took me aside and said to me, "Rick, while she was visiting this summer we noticed some changes in Polly. We think you should take her to see a doctor. We think she may be showing signs of Huntington's Disease."

I don't remember what my first reaction was. I guess it was a sense of disbelief. How could this possibly be? I agreed, however, to make an appointment with a neurologist at the University of Texas Health Science Center in Dallas.

I was a bit concerned about how Polly would react to this, so I did not tell her I was making this appointment. On the day of the appointment, I came home in the middle of the work day and said to her, "Polly, your family feels you need to see a doctor. They think you might be showing signs of HD. So I've made an appointment for today."

Our 20 minute drive across Dallas was pretty quiet. The UT Health Science Center is located adjacent to Parkland Hospital, where President John Kennedy was taken at his assassination in 1963. We parked and found our way to the doctor's office, a small "cubbyhole" of a space as I remember. He was a bespectacled young man, about thirty years of age I think. Though he would eventually become quite a specialist in working with HD patients, he later told me that Polly was only the second person he had ever examined for the illness. He was a researcher at heart, and was quite thorough in his examination of Polly. After perhaps thirty minutes he said to us, "Well, I don't see any evidence of HD in

Polly. She seems quite healthy. I think the closer she gets to forty years of age, the less you have to be concerned about." He also said that very often when people are at risk for HD they will imagine that they have it, and will even develop some minor symptoms such as awkwardness, just by the power of suggestion. This was quite a relief to us to hear. Our ride home was much more pleasant. I called her mother that evening and told her what the doctor had said. I think she was quite concerned. All I knew to do, however, was to repeat to her what the doctor had told us. I told her that I would take care of Polly and watch her closely.

Over the course of the next year, though it seemed to me that Polly was a bit quieter than usual, I didn't notice anything dramatically different about her. The following summer, however, when her mother came out to Dallas from Oregon for a visit, she suggested we take her to see the doctor again. So I made a second appointment. This time, however, he said that he saw something that caused him some concern. He asked us to come back for a much longer battery of tests. These were part of a research project he was conducting and would be carried out free of charge.

A few weeks later we appeared at his office again for the tests. Polly spent most of the day engaging in a number of activities that measured many aspects of her physiology. I distinctly remember, while we were waiting for her to be called for one of the tests to be conducted, seeing her wistfully gazing out the window. I never did ask her what she was thinking, but I really didn't need to. At the end of the day, a bit exhausted both physically and emotionally, we drove home to await his call about the results of the tests.

Several days later I was in my office at the seminary, tending to the day's tasks, when my phone rang. It was Polly. Her voice was a bit weaker than usual. "My doctor just called. He told me that... (and here her voice broke)...he's 99% sure that I do have the illness." She couldn't really say anything more. I told our department secretary that I had a personal matter to tend to at home and I drove immediately to be with her.

I don't remember well what we did the remainder of that day, or for many days after. I realized though, that from that day on our life would not be the same—and it wasn't. Just how much that would be so, I had no way of knowing.

Part 2

TWENTY YEARS
IN THE CRUCIBLE:
GOD'S PRESERVING GRACE

Chapter V

THE LIFE WE DIDN'T WANT

"No. This can't be true. There must be some other explanation." For several weeks I was convinced that Polly's symptoms were just due to stress—and so was she. We were in something of a state of denial. Over the years serving as a hospital chaplain I've observed people attempt to shake people out of denial prematurely. I've learned, however, that denial is very normal. Actually, unless it keeps someone from taking action that is urgently needed, it serves a temporary purpose. It gives us the time and space to adjust to the shock of a painful reality without being overwhelmed by it. That's why it's called a *"coping* mechanism." For a time, it helps us to cope.

When it came time for Jesus to inform his disciples of his impending betrayal and death, Peter's first response was *God forbid it, Lord! This shall never happen to You* (Mt. 16:22). How could it possibly be that the Messiah will be put to death? In the days that followed, Jesus repeated his warning at least two more times. Before He did, however, He granted his closest followers a glimpse of his future glory on the Mount of Transfiguration. He knew they would need assurance of his ultimate triumph over death which this experience must have given them. How patient and tender He was with them in the midst of their denial.

How compassionate the Lord was with us to give us an entire year between Polly's initial exam for HD and her diagnosis. Gradually though, the reality hit us that yes, she was showing signs of Huntington's Disease (HD). She was losing control of some of her fine motor skills, and would occasionally shuffle her feet or drop a plate in the kitchen.

Life seemed to move in slow motion during those initial days. Things seemed unreal and we felt somewhat numb to life. We continued to go about our daily activities, but the joy of living was muted. It seemed like we were simply going through the motions of daily life. It was a bit harder to concentrate and to think through decisions. It was harder to get to sleep at night, and to stay asleep.

Then the emotions kicked into gear—feelings of fear and uncertainty and of protest. I remember lying in bed next to Polly one night. She said to me, "Rick, what are we going to do?" I don't know what I said. There was nothing really to say. A host of questions filled our minds. How do we continue in ministry? How do we tell our children? What do we tell our friends? Most of all, why did God seemingly allow us to walk down this path to fall off this cliff? These were questions to which I had no answers.

Some people believe that Christians never have these kinds of thoughts or feelings—or at least they shouldn't have them. The fact is, however, that we do. I was encouraged some years later when I read the testimony of Joni Eareckson Tada, concerning the depression she experienced in the wake of her diving accident that left her a paraplegic for life. She wrote: "A part of the quiet rage I experienced was anger against God. Inwardly and very quietly, I raved and ranted against Him in my spirit. I think it's better to get angry at God than to walk away from Him. It's better to honestly confront our feelings and let Him know this is how we feel.... (It's) better than passing on a Colgate smile, gritting your teeth and pretending you're not hurting.... Admittedly, I felt some guilt afterward. But I was encouraged by reading examples from the Psalms. In so many, David rants and raves and just can't understand what God is doing.... The example of Jeremiah was also an encouragement. He was terribly depressed amid the horror, the battle, the invasion, the cruelty and mockery that was going on.... These examples of people in Scripture who were very real, very honest, and very human were a great encouragement. They got angry and upset and depressed. They weren't plaster saints, but real men and women who hurt and were angry and yet nonetheless held on to what they knew to be true about God from history and from His Word.... I realized these emotions were part of what it means to be human, and that to feel guilty about feelings of depression was really to feel guilty about being human."[9]

The expression of genuine human sorrow is for the most part lost on the modern church in the west. It was not lost, however, on the writers of Scripture. As I studied the Scriptures, I found Joni's words to be supported by the many passages which record the expression of genuine human sorrow. The Apostle Paul revealed that at one time he and his fellow workers were *burdened excessively, beyond* (their) *strength, so that* (they) *despaired even of life* (II Cor. 1:8b), and that he had *conflicts without, fears within* (II Cor. 7:5b).

Some may question how these emotions can be reconciled with the presence of joy, which is the fruit of God's Spirit. The Apostle Paul, however, described himself on one occasion as *sorrowful yet always rejoicing* (II Cor. 6:10a). Also in his Epistle to the Philippians, which is bathed in joy, he acknowledges that if his friend Epaphroditus had died, he would have experienced *sorrow upon sorrow* (Phil. 2:27). There is nothing inconsistent between the experience of Christian joy and the expression of genuine sorrow and lament. Likewise, we should not think that Paul's admonition in I Thessalonians 5:18 to give thanks *in everything* somehow excludes all expression of sorrow. John Stott wisely writes: "We cannot of course thank God 'for all circumstances', including those which are evil and displeasing to him; but we can and should thank him *in all circumstances....*"[10]

John Swinton writes: "The task of the practice of lament is to produce a form of character that can live with unanswered questions, not through repression or denial, but by expression and active acceptance of the reality of evil and suffering and the love of God in the midst of it. By learning the practice of lament, we become the type of people who take seriously the pain and sadness of the world but refuse to be crushed by it."[11]

Of all the psalms, probably half contain some expression of lament. Psalm 13 is a typical example of a "psalm of lament." The first two verses record an expression of complaint. *How long, O Lord? Will You forget me forever? How long will You hide your face from me?* (2) *How long shall I take counsel in my soul, Having sorrow in my heart all the day? How long will my enemy be exalted over me?* Many passages of Scripture record such expressions of sorrow from God's saints. Some people think that lament is characteristic only of Old Testament faith, and should have no place in a Christian's life. Jesus Himself, however, expressed such lament, when He said in anticipation of the cross, *Now my soul has become troubled* (Jn. 12:27a), and when on the cross He cried, *My God, my God, why have you forsaken me?* (Mt. 27:46b). Surprisingly, even the saints in heaven voice similar expressions, when they call out, *How long, O Lord, holy and true, will You refrain from judging and avenging our blood on those who dwell on the earth?* (Rev. 6:10). If such expression of lament is accepted in heaven, certainly it is acceptable on earth.

One psalm never really moves on from such an expression, Psalm 88. From beginning to end its writer does nothing but pour out his complaint to God over his affliction, which shows us that there are times when this may be all we can bring ourselves to do. Some people are offended by this. We must remember, however, (as many others have noted) that there is a big difference between complaining *to* God and complaining *against* Him. In fact, the psalmist bids us to *pour out* our heart before the Lord (Ps. 62:8).

The next two verses of Psalm 13 move from the expression of complaint to the voicing of his prayer: (3) *Consider and answer me, O Lord my God; Enlighten my eyes, or I will sleep the sleep of death,* (4) *And my enemy will say, "I have overcome him," And my adversaries will rejoice when I am shaken.* It's important that we eventually turn our lament to prayer—prayer that God might intervene in our life. We should pray until we find ourselves moving, as the psalmist does in the final two verses, to an expression of trust in the Lord: (5) *But I have trusted in Your lovingkindness; My heart shall rejoice in Your salvation.* (6) *I will sing to the Lord, Because He has dealt bountifully with me.*

Though it takes less than a minute to read Psalm 13, there are times when to move from lament, through prayer, to trust may take hours, or weeks, or months, or even longer. We may in fact find ourselves returning to this cycle more than once.

Many people turn away from God over experiences like this. It's not difficult to understand why. Nonetheless, when we choose to eliminate God from the equation of our lives, it doesn't diminish the suffering by an ounce. It does, however, certainly remove any reasonable basis for hope in the midst of our suffering.

Those who eliminate God from their view of life must resign themselves to the notion that evil and suffering are just part of the world as it is, and we must make the best of it. Those who embrace the biblical perspective, however, realize that the world is not the way God originally intended it to be. Because of the sinful rebellion of our race, God has *subjected the world to futility* (Rom. 8:20); and during this age, while we are in these mortal bodies, *we...groan within ourselves* (v. 23).

None of us can expect to escape the afflictions that sin has brought on our race. Not that one's personal sin is always the cause of one's own afflictions. Jesus taught his disciples that this is not always the case, when He responded to their question about the man born blind: *Rabbi, who sinned, this man or his parents, that he would be born blind?* (John 9:2). (Some rabbis taught that it was actually possible to sin "in the womb" and thus suffer an affliction such as blindness as a result.)[12] Jesus responded that it was neither the sin of this man or his parents that accounted for his blindness. On another occasion Jesus said of some Galileans whom the Roman governor Pilate had slaughtered, *Do you suppose that these Galileans were greater sinners than all other Galileans because they suffered this fate? .... I tell you, no, but unless you repent, you will all likewise perish* (Luke 13:2, 5). Afflictions such as these are part of our fallen human condition. Sometimes, our suffering is due to our own sin. Other times, it's due to the sins of others against us, or even to the schemes of Satan. Many times, however, it's just the result of living in this broken world.

Why, however, one person is afflicted in one way and another is not, is something we cannot know. Why was Peter delivered from prison, but James executed (Acts 12)? Why were some seemingly diverted from going into work at the Twin Towers on the morning of 9-11, but others perished when they collapsed? It is a mystery we must leave with God, until He reveals more than He has. I know that if it were not for the sin of our race, there would be no such thing as Huntington's Disease, or a host of other maladies.

Why Polly had this illness, however, and not someone else—not me—is something I do not know.

I distinctly remember one day, sitting at the table in our breakfast area, saying, "Polly, we still have to live our lives; and we still need to raise the children we love. We can't just give up and quit." We both knew that. At the same time though, we weren't quite sure how we were going to do it.

A few weeks after Polly's diagnosis, I was sitting in my office at Dallas Seminary early in the morning. It was my practice (and still is) to read a segment of Scripture in the morning. At the time, I was reading through the Psalms. That particular morning, as I was reading through Psalm 55, my eyes fell on verse 22: *Cast your burden upon the Lord and he will sustain you; He will never allow the righteous to be shaken.* It was as though these were words spoken directly by God to me. Not that we were "righteous" in ourselves. No one is. Yet I knew that we belonged to the Lord, through trusting in Christ, and these promises were for us. It was as though God was saying, "Let me carry this burden. Let me carry you. I will not let you down." As I continued reading, a few days later I came to Psalm 68:19, *Blessed be the Lord, who daily bears our burden, The God who is our salvation.*

I cannot tell you what these two verses meant to me at that time. It's been thirty years since that day, as I write these words, but my eyes are still welling up as I recall the sense of hope that God instilled in my heart that day. I had no idea *how* God would bear our burden and sustain us—but I believed that He would. I believed He would keep his word. There was no other way we could possibly navigate this unexpected journey.

Chapter VI

A NEW BEGINNING

The next few years were filled with many adjustments. We were in territory neither of us had even contemplated navigating, and there was no map or guidebook. Probably our biggest adjustment was in relating to each other. We were really going through a grieving process, though we didn't realize it at the time. We were grieving the loss of some of our hopes and dreams in life. We were grieving the loss of "normalcy." Part of grief is a feeling of protest against things that seem unfair and unjust in life.

I was protesting for one thing the fact that I was losing my wife. Though she was still alive, she was gradually becoming someone different than the girl I married. Though I loved her, and never raised my voice at her, at times I found my patience being stretched.

We were also adjusting to a change in our relationships with others. Very few of our friends and acquaintances knew anything about Huntington's, and it was impossible to inform everyone we met of what was transpiring in our lives. So people's expectations of Polly were often unrealistic. They did not understand why she was unable to do some things, or respond as quickly as she used to. I found myself wanting to avoid encounters like these and this led us to withdraw from some of the social contacts we would otherwise have enjoyed.

Some people who did learn of Polly's illness encouraged us to believe God for a miraculous healing. In fact, shortly after Polly was diagnosed, someone who had heard about it called her at home and said, "Polly, I know that if you have faith, God will heal you completely." Another friend walked up to me one day and said, "Rick, this is God's will for you." Yet another friend said, "Sometimes these things are due to some sin or spiritual problem in our life." Two fellows even told me that if we had real faith we would take Polly off all her medications and trust God to heal her.

I learned over time that such comments are usually prompted by people's desire to explain the unexplainable, and to fix the unfixable — to find answers to questions that are beyond our understanding. They are attempts to deal with the discomfort of being with someone who is in emotional or physical pain. At the worst, they may be unconscious attempts to create distance from hurting people, so as to avoid going through the trouble and inconvenience of having to relate to them. I learned in time not to take many of them very seriously, but it was not always easy to do so.

I was also adjusting to the loss of my own dreams with regard to my studies at the seminary, and future ministry. I had returned to DTS in 1981 largely out of a desire to pursue PhD studies in theology, with a view to teaching in a college or seminary. After Polly's diagnosis, however, this dream began to fade. At home, my responsibilities began to increase as Polly needed more assistance with matters of daily life. Our children, ages four and seven when Polly was diagnosed, were growing up rapidly. At work, my responsibilities were also increasing. Consequently, my progress in the PhD program slowed to a crawl. Eventually, with only the dissertation to complete, I had to abandon the dream altogether.

I realized, however, that God had apparently brought us back to DTS in part to protect us. Had Polly's diagnosis taken place while we were serving the church in the Seattle area, it would have been much more difficult for us (and very difficult for the church). At the seminary we were in somewhat of a "cocoon," where what was happening to us had only minor impact on others. I wondered, however, what I was going to do the rest of my life. How could God continue to use us in ministry?

I was meeting at that time each Friday noon with a student friend for lunch to pray. I shared with him one day that I was praying about what God wanted me to do in the future, in light of these recent events in our lives. His prayers were a great encouragement to me. He also shared with me that he was involved with a ministry through his church to international university students in our area—students who had come from other countries to study in the U.S.

Just before Polly was diagnosed, my father and I had made a three week trip to the People's Republic of China (PRC). We were guests of a former missionary to China and his family, touring much of the country and visiting some of the people whom he had not seen in some 35 years. It was an amazing and life changing experience. China had not been open to westerners very long at that time. A government assigned "guide" accompanied our group everywhere we went. Everyone was still wearing the blue "Mao jackets" and bicycles were everywhere. The few cars and trucks we saw on the road were all owned by the state. I could tell that at some of the places we went, further inland, we were an unusual spectacle.

On a few occasions we met with pastors of churches that were registered with the state. These were older men who had served time in prison in years past, but had been released and were granted permission to serve these local churches (under close watch by the government). One of them told us how during the "Cultural Revolution" they had met secretly for prayer and worship in caves and other places where their presence would not be noticed.

One day, while staying in Shanghai, we were approached by a young man who asked if he could speak English with us. Of course, we were more than happy to oblige. In the course of our conversation we learned that he was planning to come to America to study, in fact to study in San Antonio, Texas.

When we returned home, it seemed that every week I was encountering students from around the world, especially from

China. In the wake of this recent experience in China, and with the encouragement of my student friend, we decided to become involved in ministry to some of these students, simply serving as "friendship partners" to visiting scholars from the PRC. After a couple years of this kind of involvement, it seemed to us that God was redirecting us into more of a "front line" ministry than I was able to carry out at the seminary. We made application to serve with the ministry of International Students, Inc. (ISI) and were accepted. At our interview with the leadership of ISI in Colorado Springs, Polly somewhat tearfully commented to them, "If you accept us, we believe this is God's will for our life." God was giving us a new challenge and calling in life.

One of the big challenges in this ministry was the matter of raising support. This was a faith supported ministry and I had never engaged in this kind of ministry before. Though there were times when the idea of raising support to minister in this way was quite challenging, I learned that God has his ways of encouraging us when we need it.

On one occasion I was sitting at our kitchen table, addressing envelopes for a letter I was about to send to friends and prospective supporters. Just as I was addressing an envelope to a pastor friend, the phone rang. It was a call from that very individual. He said, "Rick, I'm just calling to find out how your support raising is going. I wonder if you can come to speak about your ministry at our church."

On another occasion, several months later, I was signing letters to friends. Just after signing a letter to a church in central Texas, the phone rang. It was the pastor of that church telling me that they had decided to make a commitment to our financial support.

I had told our ministry leadership that we were open to returning to the Seattle area to serve, especially as this was closer to Polly's family who lived in the Pacific Northwest. I felt that with her health in decline it might be helpful to at least not be so far away. Though we were unable to sell our home in Texas, we did rent it out, and made our way across the country to Seattle, where we began a new chapter of life.

One of our Seattle friends told us of a couple who owned a home in the Magnolia Bluff section of the city. They were in the Navy and stationed in Bahrain and needed someone to rent their home while they were gone. What a beautiful place this was for us, as we settled into life in the "Emerald City." From our living room, we actually had a dramatic view of downtown Seattle, across Elliot

Bay. What a gift of grace especially for Polly, whose health was slowly in decline.

I realized before long, that with Polly's declining health, it was a gift of God's mercy that we were engaged in a ministry with much more flexibility than I could ever have enjoyed in the structured work environment at the seminary. I had taken over all the shopping, as well as overseeing our children's progress at school. In addition, there were occasional doctor appointments for Polly. I recall on one occasion our asking her doctor about a possible change in her medication. He prescribed something that he felt would help calm her nerves. Boy did it ever. Ten minutes after giving her the first dose, she fell asleep at our dining room table during a meal. I laid her down on our sofa and she didn't wake up for eighteen hours.

The student ministry was different than anything we had done before. Our responsibilities included working with churches to help them launch outreach ministries to international students in their area, helping to plan and organize student conferences and other student related events, and engaging in personal ministry to students. God blessed this ministry in wonderful ways. Not only were many students exposed to the love of Christ through staff and volunteers who befriended them, but also to the gospel of Christ through the conferences and personal and group Bible studies. One scholar from China who attended one of our conferences said, "I will never become a Christian—but *if I do*, being at this conference will be a big reason for it."[13]

One young student from Taiwan named Li Lin lived with a family that headed up the international student outreach through their church in south Seattle. She attended a weekly Bible study for seekers that was held in their home for a number of years. It was actually after seven years of attending this study, and in the face of a personal crisis in her life, that she entrusted her life to Christ.

Our stay in Seattle, however, was to be short lived. After a year in the home on Magnolia, the owners returned from Bahrain. So it was necessary for us to find another place to rent. We did—but after two years, our landlord told us he wanted to sell the house. As we researched other options, we realized that we were really priced out of the market. Our ministry told us that we could return to Dallas if we desired. One of the local staff in Dallas was moving to another state, and there would be a place for us there. In the summer of 1990 we humbly packed up and returned to Dallas to reoccupy our home, which thankfully had not sold when we had left three years prior.

It was only a month after we returned to Dallas that I realized one evening how much trouble it was becoming for Polly to cook our family meals. Because of the shaking of her hands, it was getting quite difficult for her to manage things. I said to her that evening, "Polly, tomorrow I'm going to start preparing our family meals. I think it's getting too hard for you." Polly was not one to give up very easily. For a couple years after her diagnosis she had continued to sing in our church choir and help in the nursery. More importantly, she had continued with all the strength she had to love and care for our children. When I asked our daughter to share some of her memories of her mom from her childhood years, here is what she said: "I remember her being a devoted stay at home mom taking care of us during the days. We would drop my brother off at school and come home and play and have lunch together. I remember her putting me down in a crib for naps and picking me out. We would walk down to the end of our street to play at the park sometimes. She always loved putting holiday decorations out. I always looked forward to helping her get out the Thanksgiving and Christmas decorations. She worked hard to make Christmas special. I just remember Mom trying to plan things to help us have fun. We did swimming lessons and I remember her standing so patiently with the hose spraying us and helping us make our backyard swing-set a fun slippery wet slide. I remember Mom letting us 'cheat' when Dad went away for a day, because he wouldn't let us eat chocolate and sweets too often—ever actually! However, Dad would leave us $20 to eat dinner, and somehow my brother and I would convince Mom to let us get chocolate cookies and ice cream! Of course, I also remember her making me sit at the table for what seemed like 'hours' because I wouldn't eat my lima beans! She loved us so much and wanted us to have a fun childhood. I felt that for sure. Mom had a great all-in-one laugh (chuckle) and wink that really made her so unpretentious and warm. I feel like she really came alive and lit up when she was able to be around her family. She was so excited to host the extended family for Thanksgiving at the Seattle house when we moved there."

Polly loved being a mother to our kids and caring for our family. Yet she realized that her abilities were diminishing. Not only was it getting too difficult to cook our meals, but it was getting difficult for her to feed herself as well. Getting a fork or spoon to her mouth was becoming an increasing impossibility. So in one week's time, not only was I cooking our family meals, but I was also feeding those meals to Polly by hand.

For the next three years we continued to serve with ISI in the Dallas area. With the decline in Polly's health, however, and the increase in my caregiving, our ability to actually engage in ministry with students was becoming increasingly difficult. ISI was very kind to us during these years. They gave me the assignment of researching and writing on a number of topics relevant to the ministry, and preparing training materials and Bible studies for use in ministry to students. After a few years, however, I realized that I could not continue doing this much longer. There was only so much to write about.

Some years prior to this, while working at DTS, I had become familiar with Probe Ministries, a Christian apologetics and educational ministry. I approached them about the possibility of working with them, and they graciously welcomed us onto their team. In 1993 I became Director of Publications for Probe Ministries. My responsibilities included not only overseeing their publications ministry, but also speaking occasionally at the student conferences they conducted, and periodically writing transcripts for their five minute radio program which aired on several hundred Christian stations around the country. A number of the radio transcripts I had opportunity to write were on topics such as world religions, and the exclusivity of salvation through Christ—topics that grew out of our prior experience of working with international students.

Once again, a new chapter had begun—but in more ways than we anticipated.

Chapter VII

A NEW HOME FOR POLLY...
AND FOR ME

A year before beginning at Probe, in the spring of 1992, Polly and I were sitting in our living room, when she said to me, "Rick, I think it's time I entered a nursing home." This is a topic we had somehow avoided discussing in recent years. I think, however, that we both realized the time had come for this. Due to her problems with balance, it was unwise to leave Polly alone for long. Not only had I been cooking our meals the past couple years, and feeding her by hand, but also helping her dress, and bathe, and taking care of the rest of her personal needs. I remember several years prior, asking her neurologist when he thought it might be appropriate for us to seek out nursing home care. He said, "Well, you'll just know. You won't be able to do everything that needs to be done." I believed that time had come for us.

I hardly knew where to start in the process of finding a nursing home for Polly. The first couple of homes I visited, I noticed that everyone there seemed like they were twice her age. She was just 41 years old. It was difficult to envision her in that environment. Yet I knew she needed more care than I could provide alone. I shared with our neighbors that we were looking for a nursing home. One of them was a nurse. She and her family had taken a special interest in our daughter during her grade school years. She called me one day and told me that there was a home that had many younger residents—Brentwood Place. It was about eleven miles from our home, in a poorer area of Dallas called Pleasant Grove. It was an older facility, with four separate buildings. Each of them housed probably a hundred residents. When I visited inside, however, I felt that this was the place for her. Some of the residents were younger even than Polly—young people who had been disabled for various reasons. A few of them even took the bus each morning to classes at a community college in downtown Dallas.

Nursing home care is not free. Nor is it cheap. The only way that we could afford this kind of care for Polly was if we applied for Medicaid. We had never thought about obtaining long term care insurance at our age in life; and with her disability, there is no way she would have been approved. So we made an appointment with the Texas Department of Health and Human Services for her to be interviewed.

At the interview, the staff person told us, "For Polly to be approved for Medicaid, there are two primary qualifications. The first is that she must be disabled. The second is that your total financial assets must fall under the cap established by the state of Texas." During the interview, it became evident to the staff person that due to her disabilities, Polly did qualify for Medicaid assistance. When we totaled our assets, they fell just under the cap by a few hundred dollars if I remember.

A few months later I realized that if we had waited one more month to apply for Medicaid, our assets would have exceeded the cap and Polly would have been denied coverage. At that time in the state of Texas, if you applied for Medicaid and were denied due to your assets exceeding the cap, you could not apply again for two years. I'm not sure how we would have survived another two years without the assistance that enabled her to take up residence at Brentwood Place. I had sometimes wondered why God had seemed to keep us quite so poor over the years. Now I knew one reason why He did. This was God's time, and God's provision, for Polly. Hardly a "mere coincidence."

I will never forget the first day that Polly took up residence at Brentwood Place. As we approached the nurses' station in the middle of the building, Polly smiled and greeted one of the nurses, "Hi. I'm Polly. I'm new." I could tell the staff was pleased to have Polly there.

We were directed down her hall to what would be her room—a small, probably twelve by fifteen foot room that she would share with a roommate (an elderly lady who had been there for some time already). There was a dresser, a closet, two single beds and a small bathroom. I put her clothes in her dresser and closet and went down the hall to the dining room to share lunch with her. As I looked around at a room full of what seemed to me incredibly disabled people, I realized that we were entering a very different world than we had ever known. Some were drooling. Others were mumbling to themselves. Most were just quietly sitting, waiting for their meal to be served. One of the tables was especially reserved for residents who needed to have their meals fed to them by hand. This would become Polly's table too.

After bringing her back to her room, I gave her a hug and I told her I would return the next day. Walking out the front door to my car, I looked back at what I believed would be my wife's home for the rest of her life. My heart was filled with a mixture of gratitude and grief. I was grateful for the care she would receive here. The staff here could do far more for her than I could possibly do alone. Yet I was also grieving for her, that her life had finally come to the place of needing this much care.

At first, I had planned to visit Polly every other evening, and to bring her home on the weekends. For a couple weeks I think this is what I did. The social worker shared with me one day, however, that Polly seemed depressed the evenings I wasn't there. I decided that I was going to go every night, and that's exactly what I did. After preparing dinner for my children, and trying to see that they started on their homework, I drove to Polly's home for about an hour's visit, returning home about 9:00pm.

Many people are reluctant to seek nursing home care for their loved one—and I can understand why. Even the most conscientious nursing home staff is no substitute for a family. There are times, however, when it's impossible (along with all the other responsibilities in life) to provide all the care a loved one needs. When this is the case, a nursing home can be a wonderful blessing. Prior to Polly's entering the nursing home, it seemed that we were doing all we could just to survive. Now we had the help of an entire staff with many of those responsibilities.

Nonetheless, it's important for us as family to remember that in spite of the assistance of the nursing home staff, we are still our loved one's primary caregiver. We are responsible for their well-being. It's an unfortunate fact that not all families see things this way. In fact, I read one study that stated that 60% of nursing home residents do not receive regular visits from their family—or from anyone else.[14] This is a shameful truth. Certainly, there are some caregivers who neglect to care for themselves and they burn out taking care of their loved one and even become seriously ill. There are others, however, who fail to take seriously the responsibility they have, and who forfeit many of the joys of sharing life with the one God has given them to love.

It was a joy to see Polly every night; and it seemed to mean so much to her. Polly was using a walker at that time. We would walk down the hall to sit at a table to talk about our day. I would usually get her an iced tea to sip through a straw. Sometimes we would walk outside to sit on a bench beneath a tree on the property. It was a good and quiet place for us to talk and pray together. We prayed about our days. Most of all, we prayed for our children. For many years Polly had made it a practice to read from her Bible on her own each day. One time, while she was still residing at home, and when her fears about her life were troubling her, I printed some Scripture passages on some note cards and attached them to our refrigerator door. I remember seeing her standing there reading them to herself. In the nursing home we began the practice of reading the Bible together—or I should say, that I began reading the Bible to her. It was a practice we never gave up.

Many activities are planned for nursing home residents. One of Polly's favorites was "balloon volleyball." You can imagine what this was like. The dining room was cleared for the two opposing teams of residents seated in their chairs or wheelchairs, batting a balloon across the room—laughing and enjoying the simplest of activities. When special dinners were planned for holidays such as Thanksgiving and Christmas, many family members would come. I would bring one of Polly's nicest dresses, and we would walk down the hall to the dining room to enjoy a special dinner and entertainment. The latter was usually provided by local talent who volunteered their time. The head administrator of Brentwood Place even had his own band, and they would perform from time to time.

When we first entered the nursing home, I wondered if we would ever adjust to living in this environment. I can tell you that in time, the nursing home became my second home, and the residents and staff became my second family. For the most part, the people residing there had been reduced to their basic human essence. They had nothing to prove and nothing to lose. I learned to love them dearly. I miss nursing home life very much.

Shortly after Polly entered the nursing home, she turned to me and said, "Do you think I should start witnessing to the other residents about the Lord?" To say that my heart was touched by this question would be an understatement. It reflected the simple, genuine faith that Polly had. She realized that God had placed her here for a purpose; and she wanted to be faithful to Him. Indeed, Polly was a faithful witness for the Lord—if not so much by her words, yet very much so by her life. Years later I would have occasion to ask staff at the nursing home to record their memories of Polly. I will share some of those later.

In spite of these events, nursing home life can become pretty routine, and at times discouraging. So I decided early on that I would plan some kind of outing with Polly once or twice a week. Weekends she came home with me; and during the football and basketball seasons at our children's high school, we made it a practice to attend virtually every game—even the away games.

Our son played football during three of his high school years, and we went to all his games together. I remember one time driving Polly all the way from Dallas to Austin, about 200 miles away, to watch a game our son played in. It was cold, and we sat in the stands bundled in a heavy blanket. Polly's enjoyment of these sporting events was a reflection of her devotion as a mother and of her intense love for our children. I can still hear her voice, cheering for our son, "Let's go son!"

Good movies, Christian concerts, sporting events, the Texas State Fair—these were some of the events that gave Polly something to look forward to each week. I remember well pushing her in her wheelchair through the State Fairgrounds in Dallas each October. She seemed to especially love the smaller farm animals that she could reach out and touch. I think it reminded her of her childhood days in Oregon, when her family owned some livestock on their rural property. On one occasion I brought her to the Six Flags amusement park near Dallas. Lifting her from her wheelchair I sat her in a small boat that travelled down a pretty fast waterway. When we got to the end, she said, "Let's go again." For a few summers I brought her about once a month to see the Texas Rangers baseball club play in Arlington. We generally sat in the outfield. Some of the attendants got to know us fairly well from our monthly visits to the same section. It didn't really matter if we could see everything. It was just such a pleasure to know that she was enjoying herself. On a few occasions I took Polly to see the Dallas Mavericks NBA basketball team play. We were permitted to sit in the wheelchair section where we paid only five or ten dollars—much cheaper than the seats right in front of us.

For several years, we made it our practice to sit at the back of our church sanctuary Sunday mornings—Polly in her wheel chair and I sitting beside her. It may seem self-serving to say this—and maybe it is. Yet I will never forget Polly telling me one day, "Rick, you help make my life worthwhile." Just hearing her say that told me all I needed to know.

Still, I would be less than honest if I said that we did not endure times of doubt and discouragement. When Polly entered the nursing home, I had no idea how long she would be there, or how long she would live. As the years had gone by, we had also grown apart from our network of friends. I've observed over the years that when a person becomes ill, there is usually a great deal of support at the beginning. However, when an illness drags on for years, and the person grows more and more disabled, most friends drift away.

It is not uncommon as well, for a disabled individual to experience becoming somewhat of an "invisible" person even when in public. Often when I would take Polly out to public places and events, very few people would acknowledge her presence. Some would obviously avoid making eye contact. At first it was a very uncomfortable feeling.

Even among those who knew us, there seemed to be a reluctance to engage Polly in any meaningful way. One friend said to me one day, "Rick, we just can't relate to Polly. You can, but we just can't." I don't remember saying anything, but I do remember wondering if he had ever really tried. It's unfortunate that in our culture, the disabled, the disfigured, and the dying are largely hidden away from view. Many of them reside in institutions or homes where they have little contact with the outside world. Whereas there was a day when most people grew old and died at home, in America this is no longer usually the case. Consequently, many of us grow up having little if any opportunity to learn to relate well to those who fall outside the boundaries of what we have come to think of as a "normal" life.

Some parents seem to go to great lengths to shelter their children from exposure to people or circumstances outside the parameters of "normalcy." Little do they realize that by doing so they are depriving them of the very experiences that will instill in them the empathy and compassion they themselves may one day desperately need from others, and which will help them grow into mature men and women who recognize that the blessings they have in life are not "entitlements," but are gifts of God's mercy. They are gifts for which to be grateful, and to be used in humble service to Him and to others. The wise parent will take initiative in making sure their children are appropriately exposed to the world as it really is—not as we would like it to be.

I remember one day reading through the prophet Isaiah. I came to this description of the Lord's Servant: *He was despised and forsaken of men, a man of sorrows and acquainted with grief; and like one from whom men hide their face He was despised, and we did not esteem Him* (Isa. 53:3). This is a prophetic description of the Messiah Jesus, particularly of his appearance as a result of the severe beating He received prior to his going to the cross. Yet it told me that He knows exactly how many people in this world feel.

James says that *Pure and undefiled religion in the sight of our God and Father is this: to visit orphans and widows in their distress* (those most vulnerable in that day), *and to keep oneself unstained by the world* (James 1:27). To "visit" means more than to occasionally drop by and wish someone well. It means to come to their aid—to ask God how we can best serve their greatest good. Pastoral theologian John Swinton writes: "The term 'visit' has its origins in the Latin word 'videre,' meaning 'to see, notice, or observe' (hence the word 'video'). To visit someone is to see them.... It is as we visit one another that we learn the true meaning of the words, 'It's good that you exist; it's good that you are in this world.'"[15]

When we stand before the Lord Jesus, one of the tests by which He will measure the genuineness of our spiritual profession is whether we have demonstrated our love by visiting *the least* of his spiritual family (Matt. 25:40).

Certainly, part of our ministry to the sick and suffering is to pray for their healing in the will of God. Indeed, we do rejoice when God manifests his extraordinary works of mercy. Is this, though, the full extent of what love requires? A brother in Africa once said to me, "I've seen Christians who persistently pray for the healing of the sick, but when God doesn't seem to be answering their prayers as they would like, they just move on to someone else until someone is healed." Is this really the way the Lord would have us conduct ourselves toward the sick and suffering?

Jesus said that *many* who claim to have performed miracles in his name (including miracles of healing) will be turned away from entering his kingdom on the day of judgment (Mt. 7:22-23). Prominent, however, among those whom He will welcome into his kingdom will be those to whom He will be able to say *I was sick and you visited Me* (Mt. 25:36).

Please don't misunderstand what I am saying. I rejoice as much as anyone when God intervenes to reverse the course of an illness, or to remove the cause of suffering. There are times when He certainly does. However, this is not all that God is doing in this world. He is also helping many of his children to give evidence of his grace as He carries them *through* their trials, some of which may last an entire lifetime. Some of the grace God provides to the suffering comes through the compassionate love of brothers and sisters who take the time and trouble to show that they truly care. In the next chapter I share some thoughts on ways we might do just that.

Chapter VIII

HELPING THE SUFFERING

O ver the years of living with Polly, and then for many years serving also as a hospital chaplain, I've been forced to reflect on what it takes to truly care for the suffering. I can't claim that I've always lived up to what I will write in this chapter. Yet I want to pass on some of the thoughts that have been impressed on my heart over the years, by simply listing several groups of scripture passages along important themes and making a few comments based on them.

*(A)dmonish the unruly, **encourage** the fainthearted, **help** the weak, be **patient** with everyone* (I Thess. 5:14). *For the despairing man there should be **kindness** from his friend;*

so that he does not forsake the fear of the Almighty (Job 6:14). (Emphasis my own.)

In caring for the suffering, the goal is to be encouraging, helpful, patient and kind. It sounds so easy. Yet if you are like me, you know that it isn't always so. Often we feel it's much easier to simply avoid getting involved—or even to be irritated by those whose suffering upsets our quest for a tranquil life. This is not the way God calls us to go. I know as well as any, that if we are to go his way, we need Him to help us. We need to ask Him to instill in our hearts these very qualities and to help us grow in living them out.

This doesn't come by waiting until we *feel* particularly helpful or patient or kind. It comes as we exercise helpfulness, patience and kindness in the concrete relationships and in the circumstances of our daily lives. It comes by prayerful practice. At first it may not seem natural or comfortable to get involved in the life of someone who is suffering. However, as we ask God for his grace, and then as we begin to do what we know needs to be done, we gradually find God causing us to grow in these qualities. How many times have I needed to ask God to help me simply be more patient and kind—and I still do.

> **Weep** *with those who weep, and rejoice with those who rejoice* (Rom. 12:15). *Like one who takes off a garment on a cold day, or like vinegar on soda, is he who sings songs to a troubled heart* (Prov. 25:20).

Empathy is the ability to enter into the emotional suffering of another person. According to the Bible, it's a virtue that characterizes God Himself. Speaking of Israel in her sufferings, God says, *In all their affliction, I was afflicted* (Isa. 63:9). Jesus is spoken of as a *High Priest* who is able to *sympathize with our weaknesses* (Heb. 4:14-16). Empathy is something that seems to come naturally to some (though not to all). It is a quality that I frequently find myself asking God to instill in my heart as I talk with patients, as only He can do. Rarely will we be able to feel exactly what another person feels; and we should avoid telling someone who is suffering that we do. We can, however, certainly try to understand how they feel. This is where empathy begins.

The consequence of failing to empathize with the suffering is illustrated in the Proverb cited here. It tells us that we should not be surprised at the severe reaction, when rather than empathizing, we seek to impose a kind of "forced cheerfulness" on someone who is suffering. It's like pulling off someone's jacket in sub-zero weather, or pouring vinegar on baking soda. Not something we would want someone to do to us.

*Like apples of gold in settings of silver is a **word** spoken in right circumstances* (Prov. 25:11). *I have many **words** to tell you, but you cannot bear them now* (John 16:12). *The Lord God has given Me the tongue of disciples, that I may know how to sustain the weary one with a **word**. He awakens Me morning by morning, He awakens My ear to listen as a disciple* (Isa. 50:4).

Words can bring either healing or pain, depending on which ones we use (as well as which ones we don't), and on how (and when) we use them. Part of wisdom is knowing how to use words in an appropriate way, and at an appropriate time, especially with the suffering. Often I find myself speaking without thinking, or at least being tempted to do so—hopefully less now than before. Yet once spoken, our words cannot really be taken back. Jesus' statement from John is instructive. Shortly before his death, He told his disciples that He had much more to tell them. He knew, however, that it would need to wait—to wait until their hearts were prepared by the Holy Spirit to receive what He had to say. He knew when to speak and when not to. I need wisdom to do the same. The statement from Isaiah teaches us that the ability to use words in such a way as to uplift and sustain is acquired as we take time first to listen to the Lord as He speaks to us through his Word, each and every day.

One of the ways in which we use words wisely is by avoiding trying to give simple solutions to people's problems, or trying to explain why someone is suffering as they are. A chaplain who helped to train me for work in the hospital said to me one day, "Rick, when a patient asks the question 'why?' it's usually not a theological question. It's a cry for understanding."[16] There is a place for discussing why God might allow evil and suffering, but it is usually not at someone's bedside.

*Be quick to **hear**, slow to speak, slow to anger* (James 1:19). *Then they sat down on the ground with him for seven days and seven nights **with no one speaking a word to him**, for they saw that his pain was very great* (Job 2:13). *O that you would be completely **silent**, and that it would become your wisdom!.... Be **silent** before me so that I may speak, then let come on me what may* (Job 13:5, 13).

Sometimes (more often than we think) the best thing we can do for someone (particularly when they are in the crucible of emotional pain) is to simply listen to them. Or, if they are in too much pain to even speak, our own quiet presence is the best gift we can give them at such a moment. I often find myself thinking that to be helpful I need to be *doing* something, or *saying* something, when the best thing I can do is simply be there and listen. When we listen, we are giving someone the gift of understanding and love. The better we listen, the more able we will also be to focus our prayers on the person's real needs.[17]

Many of us who are in vocational ministry find it difficult to refrain from speaking. We are trained to preach and teach. There is a time, however, to restrain our speech, and to simply listen. It's one of the most important things we can learn to do; and it's just as much a skill to be learned and cultivated as is speaking.[18]

I cannot count the times when patients in the hospital have said to me, "Thank you so much just for listening." The first time I was present at the passing of a patient in the hospital, at the end of the day their family said to me, "Thank you for all you've done." I really had done little more than simply be with them and listen to them. What a balm such a quiet presence and listening ear can be to someone who is suffering.

For whatever was written in earlier times was written for our instruction, so that through perseverance and the **encouragement of the Scriptures** *we might have hope* (Rom. 15:4). *Let the* **word of Christ** *richly dwell within you, with all wisdom teaching and admonishing one another with psalms and hymns and spiritual songs....* (Colossians 3:16).

When we're suffering, the Scriptures can bring hope and encourage us in such a way that we can persevere when we feel like quitting. Vaclav Havel wrote: "Hope is...not the conviction that something will turn out well, but the certainty that something makes sense, no matter how it turns out."[19] Even if now *we* do not see clearly what sense it makes, God does. Certainly, for the believer, all things will ultimately turn out well—but they may not seem to in this lifetime. Part of ministering to the suffering is knowing how to use God's Word in such a way that it accomplishes this desired effect—that it instills this kind of hope in the suffering. Many have observed that it's usually *after* a person has been listened to, and their emotions have been expressed, that they are more able to truly hear and reflect on God's Word. Sometimes we interject Scripture prematurely, when we should be listening. If, however, we are patient and we carefully listen to our suffering friend, it will become evident when they might be receptive to reading something that will help them reflect biblically and theologically on their experience. This is when the soil of their heart will most likely be receptive to the sowing of God's Word. It's important, however, that we always refrain from "preaching" to those who are in pain. There are better ways to gently plant the seed of God's truth in the tender soil of their heart. Sometimes it's appropriate to simply ask them what God is teaching them through this experience. We can learn a great deal from listening to what they may have to say.[20]

There are several ways in which Scripture can bring encouragement to the suffering. Reading through the many examples of people whose afflictions are recorded in the Bible can be a great encouragement to us: the examples of Joseph, Job, Jeremiah, Paul and Jesus Himself. Meditating on God's promises to be with us, to strengthen and comfort us, can encourage us (e.g. Isa. 41:10, 13). Being reminded that our present afflictions are temporary, and that a wonderful glory awaits us in the future can strengthen our hearts (e.g. II Cor. 4:17-18), as can those passages which tell us that God can use our present sufferings to accomplish his purposes in our lives (e.g. II Cor. 4:16; Rom. 5:3-4).

First, however, Christ's words must *dwell richly* and deeply in our own hearts. We must take time each day to bathe our minds in the Word of God, so that when the opportunity arises, we will be able to direct our friend to an appropriate Scripture. I have learned the hard way how important it is that before attempting to minister God's words to others, I take time to let them minister deeply to me.

*You also joining in helping us through your **prayers**, so that thanks may be given by many persons on our behalf for the favor bestowed on us through the **prayers** of many (II Cor. 1:11). Now I urge you, brethren, by our Lord Jesus Christ and by the love of the Spirit, to strive together with me in your **prayers** to God for me.... (Rom. 15:30). Is any among you suffering? Then he must **pray** (James 5:13a).*

Perhaps the most important thing we can do for anyone who is suffering is to pray for them, and when possible to pray *with* them. If there is anything God has done for me all these years in the hospitals, it's to teach me how indispensable it is to give myself to prayer—for myself, as well as for and with others. In the hospital I almost always ask if a patient would like me to pray with them, or to pray for them on my own. I will never forget visiting a patient many years ago and praying with him. Before I left he said to me, "You don't remember me, do you? I was here a few months ago. You stopped by to see me for just a few minutes, but you prayed with me. You know, your prayer prompted me to reevaluate my relationship with God; and the past few months have been different." I would have never known.

As the Romans text above suggests, prayer is a struggle. It is for me. I struggle in prayer—not with God, but against my own spiritual weakness, as well as against the spiritual adversaries who will do everything and anything to keep me from it. How thankful I am that part of my every day "job" is to pray with many people— not just for their sake, but for my own as well.

*Little children, let us not **love** with word or with tongue, but in deed and truth* (I John 3:18).

A fitting way to close this section is to be reminded that all we do be done in love. Love can be communicated in words, but it is most powerfully shown in our actions. Few of us will have opportunity to offer "great" acts of love for others. As Mother Teresa is reported to have said, "In this life we cannot do great things. We can only do small things with great love."[21] Pascal made the following statement: "Do small things as if they were great, because of the majesty of Christ, who does them in us and lives our life, and great things as if they were small and easy, because of his almighty power."[22]

During the years of caring for Polly I noticed that with each passing year, my love and concern for her seemed to be focused on increasingly smaller aspect of her life. At the end, it was simply washing her face or giving her a small drop of juice to taste that made the difference in her day. At times I found myself recalling the words of Jesus about the value of giving a cup of water in his name to the one who is thirsty (Mt. 10:42).

Some years ago I sat down and wrote out some of the lessons I felt the Lord had been teaching me through the first decade of ministry in the hospitals. Here are some that came to mind.

That the most significant need any patient of family member has is for a vital relationship with Christ.

That God uses weak and fallible vessels like me in his work in people's lives.

That the most important thing I can do before ministering to others is to tend to my own spiritual wellbeing.

That though I can't do everything for everybody, I can do *something* for everyone God brings across my path—if only to pray for them.

That I will never stop needing to grow, personally and spiritually.

That even the smallest of life's blessings is worthy of our thanks.

That every patient is worthy of my undivided attention.

That being in ministry is a gift of God's grace, from beginning to end.

That just being present when people are in pain is a means of grace.

That quietly listening to people's stories may be one of the best gifts I can give them.

That prayer can accomplish far more than we will ever know.

That God's Word truly does bring light in the darkness, hope to the despairing.

That the most important day of our life is today.

That it's the little things, not the "great" things we do that matter most.

That words have the power to bring either healing or pain.

That when we get to the end of our life, it's our relationships with people and with the Lord that will matter most of all.

Over the years, I've noticed that two qualities seem to be required above all others for those who would minister to the suffering. The first is the experience of suffering itself. In time, affliction can have a tenderizing effect if we let it, that enables us to empathize with others who are in pain—and empathy and compassion are indispensable ingredients in ministry. The second, however, is the experience of the grace of God. It's our experience of God's grace in our own troubles that qualifies us to encourage others, and to point them to the source of all genuine comfort and hope. It's to a discussion of God's comfort in affliction that I will turn in the next chapter.

Chapter IX

THE GOD OF ALL COMFORT

The Apostle Paul uses some beautiful words in describing our God in the opening verses of his Second Letter to the Corinthians: *Blessed be the God and Father of our Lord Jesus Christ, the Father of mercies and God of all comfort, who comforts us in all our affliction* (II Cor. 1:3-4a). I knew that God understood as no one else could exactly what we were experiencing; and over the years, He had many ways of encouraging us. I want to share some of them in this chapter.

One day while sitting in my office at Probe Ministries, one of my co-workers brought me a package that had come in the mail that day for me. He said to me quietly, "Rick, I think you'll be interested in this." As I opened it, I discovered it was a book, with a letter from the authors. The authors had sent this book to us, asking if we would consider marketing it to our constituency. This is the only request of this nature that I remember receiving while I served at Probe. As I examined the book, I realized that it was a story about a married couple who lived in Longview, Texas. Why the authors sent such a book as this to Probe, an apologetics ministry, I do not know. As I glanced through the book, I noticed something that caught my attention. This was the story of a wife whose husband had Huntington's Disease (HD)—Polly's rare illness. (We later met the woman whose story is recounted in this book. We were blessed to get to know her, as well as by the story told in the book.) The authors did not know me, or anything about Polly's illness. I believe the Lord urged them to send it to us, as a means of encouragement. Hardly a "mere coincidence."

Earlier in our journey, a few years before she entered the nursing home, Polly and I were given the opportunity of going to Washington D.C., where she participated in a study on HD at the National Institutes of Health. We had one day during our stay there when we had time to take the train downtown to see some of the sights. While we were approaching the Washington Monument who should we encounter but Polly's step-sister Bonnie and her children from Portland, Oregon. They also happened to be visiting Washington D. C. She didn't even know that we were there, but our paths crossed at the right time and the right place for us to enjoy a friendly visit over lunch.

About five years after entering the nursing home, it became evident that Polly's ability to eat was becoming seriously compromised. The medical staff asked that Polly have some tests done to determine the extent of her ability to swallow food. As a result of these tests, they asked that Polly consider going on a permanent feeding tube. The social worker came to her room to talk with us about this. She said, "Polly, take a couple days to think about this, and let us know what you want to do." This is a pretty big decision for anyone to make. It involves giving up eating and drinking for the rest of one's life. We had only a couple days to make this decision.

I knew that this was Polly's decision to make, but I wanted to be the best encouragement to her I could be. The next morning, while conducting my rounds at the hospital where I had been serving as chaplain the previous year or so, I entered one room on the third floor to discover a female patient, and her husband sitting in a chair next to her bed. I introduced myself, and told them

I was seeing everyone on the floor. (I learned early on in hospital ministry the importance of telling them this, so that they don't think I'm singling them out for a special visit. This can be a bit startling for some patients.) As I talked with this couple, I learned that the wife had recently made the same decision that Polly was being confronted with regarding a feeding tube. She was in the hospital to have the tube inserted. What surprised me, though, was that this woman told me she had the very same illness Polly had— Huntington's Disease. I generally see people with her illness in the hospital only once every year or two, but I saw her on the exact day that I needed some encouragement with regard to Polly's decision!

One Saturday evening, after reading from Isaiah 6 to Polly at her bedside, I left the nursing home to attend a worship service at a nearby church. As the pastor began his message, he announced his text. It was the very passage I had just read to Polly, Isaiah chapter 6.

During these days, our finances remained pretty marginal. We had just enough to get by in life. This caused me some concern especially during our children's teenage years, when many unexpected expenses arose. I well remember feeling convinced that our son would benefit from braces for his teeth. He had a gap between his upper front teeth; and he was so self-conscious about it that he would rarely smile. I wanted to do something about it, but our income was such that I was hesitant to commit to the expense. So we prayed about it. I decided to take him to the orthodontist to see what it would cost to help him. The total cost would be in excess of $3,000. The charge for the initial exam was $270. Believe it or not, this was no small amount for us during those days. I prayed that God would provide for this, because I felt that he really needed it. Yet I didn't want to presume on God by taking on an obligation that seemed beyond our means at the time.

Over the following weeks I saved up the $270, and made an appointment to see the orthodontist. I was hoping the Lord would give me some kind of encouragement that He would provide for this. On the very day that I took our son for his exam, three letters from three different people in various parts of the country arrived in our mail box. Each of them contained a check. One of the checks was for $200. The next one was for $60. The third check was for $10. They totaled exactly $270. The two larger checks were personal gifts, for no reason in particular. None of them knew anything about our financial concerns. Need I say more? He got his braces—and eventually, his smile returned.

This is not to say that I believe we should just sit back and expect God to fill our mailbox with checks. He normally provides for us through our work and our frugality. We must remember, however, that everything ultimately comes from Him; and at times, He reminds us of this in unmistakable and extraordinary ways. This was one of those times and one of the many ways that the Lord encouraged us during this long journey.

Many of our friends encouraged us along the way as well. What would we have done without them? Countless friends, including people at our church, upheld us in prayer. They did what they could to express their concern. Some of the ladies in the church made a beautiful blanket for Polly, with matching pillow. "I love it" was Polly's response. On one occasion, I asked if friends would send cards to Polly on her birthday. I felt it would be an encouragement to her. What a response she received. Scores and scores of people sent her their greetings.

Two ladies in particular, our neighbor Jeane Olson, and her friend Claire Lorret, visited Polly once a month for several years. We will be forever grateful for our dear church family and friends. I must not neglect to mention Polly's mother who, while she lived several years in neighboring Arkansas caring for her own mother, came monthly to Dallas to spend a weekend with Polly. She was a source of great joy and encouragement to her. These friends and family members were God's *hands and feet*, agents of his mercy and love.

The important thing was that God understood us, and He was with us. In my own Scripture reading during those years, I frequently noted that when God's people endured unusual hardship, He was with them in a special way. When Joseph was in slavery, and then in prison, the text says, *But the Lord was **with** Joseph* (Gen. 39:2, 21). When the Apostle Paul faced trial before Nero, he said, *At my first defense no one supported me but all deserted me.... But the Lord stood **with** me and strengthened me....* (II Tim. 4:16-17a). When Daniel's three friends were cast into the fiery furnace, they remained unharmed, because there was One *with* them *like a son of the gods* (Dan. 3:25). When Israel was in exile, the Lord said to the nation: *Do not fear, for I am **with** you; Do not anxiously look about you, for I am your God, I will strengthen you, surely I will help you, Surely I will uphold you with My righteous right hand* (Isa. 41:10).

Even if the rugged terrain we are traversing in life is due (in whole or in part) to our own waywardness and sin, I believe that if we turn to God with a repentant and humble heart, He will be with us and help us through the consequences of our sin. When Adam and Eve disobeyed God, they suffered the results of their sin. However, when they humbly confessed their sin, God not only forgave them, but He provided *garments of skin* for them, *and clothed them* (Gen. 3:21). When the nation Israel disobeyed God and refused to enter the land He had promised them, they too suffered the consequence, being forbidden to enter the land until an entire generation had perished (Num. 14). Yet, because they were his people and Moses interceded for them, God provided for them and cared for them all the years they spent in the wilderness. In fact, as the next generation prepared to enter the land, the Lord said to them, *I have led you forty years in the wilderness; your clothes have not worn out on you, and your sandal has not worn out on your foot* (Deut. 29:5).

In our own life, I was learning that though God may call on us to endure affliction not of our choosing, He will never call on us to endure it alone. *Even though I walk through the valley of the shadow of death, I fear no evil, for You are **with** me....* (Psalm 23:4).

The events that I've recorded in this chapter I learned to see as evidences of God's presence with us. There were just too many of them to continue to call them "mere coincidences." We have a word in Christian theology that kind of rhymes with the word "coincidence." It's the word "providence." If you look in the dictionary, you will find that the English word providence comes from the verb "to provide." This word is based on two Latin words: the preposition *pro* (forward) and the verb *videre* (to watch, or see). One aspect of God's providence is his seeing in advance what will be needed to fulfill his purpose for us, and his *making provision* for us. It is by God's providence that He works things *together* for our ultimate good. I don't pretend to know *how* He does it, but I am persuaded that He does— and *this* makes all the difference in the world.

Of course, God used his word to comfort and encourage us throughout these years; and there was one passage of Scripture that He used more than any other. The next chapter is devoted to this beloved passage.

Chapter X

THE LORD, OUR SHEPHERD

W hen Polly moved into the nursing home, our daughter gave us a large sized copy of the 23rd Psalm, which I hung on the wall by her bed. It was a daily reminder that though our life had taken a very difficult turn, the Lord was with us, and He had promised to shepherd us the remainder of our days on earth. I have studied and meditated on this psalm hundreds of times in the years since placing it on her wall. I want to share in this chapter some of my thoughts on this most familiar and precious of psalms.[23]

A. W. Tozer wrote that "What comes into our minds when we think about God is the most important thing about us."[24] I believe it's true. If we think of God as distant and uninvolved with our lives, this will shape how we live out our days. If we think of God as intimately involved with every detail of our lives, this will turn our lives in a much different direction.

Our perceptions of God are shaped by many things. They're shaped by our relationships with people who may have "represented" God to us. They're shaped by experiences in life, both good and bad. They're shaped by our own desires of what we would like God to be—even if He is not. It's important that our conceptions of God be shaped by how He has revealed Himself to actually be. That's why it's important that we listen carefully to what the Bible teaches us about what God is like.

One of the ways the Bible teaches us about God is through his names. He is called *El Shaddai*, "Almighty God." He is called *El Elyon*, "Most High God." *El Olam*, "The Everlasting God." *El Roi*, "The God who Sees Me." *Jehovah Jireh*, "The God who Provides." *Jehovah Sabbaoth*, "The Lord of Hosts." The names of God tell us much about who He is and what He is like.[25]

The Bible also teaches us something about God through its metaphors or figures of speech. God is our "fortress," our "rock," our "shield." The metaphor that is most frequently used, however, and which teaches us perhaps more than any other, is the one used in this psalm. The Lord is our "shepherd." The first person in the Bible to call God his shepherd was Jacob. In blessing his son Joseph, he said, *God...has been my shepherd all my life to this day* (Gen. 48:16).[26]

There is no passage that unlocks for us the relationship we have with the Lord as our shepherd, like this one. This is a psalm of David. David himself had been a shepherd over his father's flocks; and as king, he had shepherded the Lord's people as a nation. He knew whereof he was speaking. It's likely that David wrote this psalm during a time of distress, perhaps even while he was separated from the Lord's "house" in Jerusalem—the place of worship and fellowship with God. It was during such a time that he reflected on the fact that no matter what was occurring in his life, the Lord was his shepherd.

The psalm begins with a statement of its theme: *The Lord is my shepherd, I shall not want.* It's humbling to acknowledge that the Lord is our shepherd, because it implies that we are not unlike sheep; and the Bible is not too flattering in its description of sheep. *All of us like sheep have gone astray, each of us has turned to his own way* (Isa. 53:6a). Sheep are prone to wander. In fact, someone has expressed wonder that sheep could ever have survived in the wild without a shepherd. Talk about the "survival of the fittest." The survival of sheep would seem to invalidate the entire concept.[27] Yes, it's humbling to acknowledge that we are nothing but sheep, desperately in need of a shepherd.

However, this statement is also very encouraging, because it tells us that the One who is our shepherd is the One who made us and knows us. He knows us intimately and individually. *The Lord is **my** shepherd*. He knows us better than anyone else—even better than we know ourselves. He knows exactly what we need. That's why it says that if the Lord is our shepherd, we *shall not want*. That is, we shall not be in want of or lack what He knows we truly need. Of course, this does not mean He will give us whatever we desire, or think that we need.[28] His wisdom is far superior to our own.

As I read the psalm, it falls into three sections, each one defining an aspect of how the Lord shepherds our lives. First, **the Lord is our shepherd in the daily rhythm of life**. Note verses two and three: *He makes me lie down in green pastures; He leads me beside quiet waters. He restores my soul; He guides me in the paths of righteousness For His name's sake.*

This is a good description of the daily life of a flock in Palestine. Notice that there are two phases in this daily rhythm. There is time in the pasture and there is time on the pathway. In the pasture we see the flock being rested, nourished, cleansed and renewed. Sheep need pasture and water. The word used here for green pastures signifies the lush grassy meadows of springtime—the best kind of pasture to graze in.[29] The quiet, still waters are also the best kind not only for drinking, but also for bathing and cleansing.[30] As a result, the sheep are *restored* or returned to a state of wellbeing. These are the basic daily needs of sheep. They are our basic needs as well—not only physically, but spiritually. Perhaps we might see here our daily need for spiritual nourishment through God's Word, as well as cleansing from sin through God's grace, so that we are restored and refreshed.[31] As our faithful shepherd, the Lord knows that this is what we need most of all; and it is to our detriment that we ignore his daily provisions.

Need I say that during our long journey together, Polly and I learned anew how deeply we needed God's daily spiritual nourishment and cleansing. Reading through the Scriptures and taking time for prayer were essential to our spiritual survival. At times, prayer became a struggle for me personally, and I often found help in actually writing out my prayers in full sentences and logging them in a notebook.

The other side of this daily rhythm is time on the pathway. When a flock had finished grazing in one pasture, the shepherd would guide them to another—and he knew the right path to get there. The word for *path* here is literally "wagon tracks."[32] These tracks would mark the way to the proper destination. Note that the path is designated as a *righteous* path. The Lord will always guide us in righteous ways. He does so primarily through his Word (though He may also employ godly counsel, as well as providential circumstance). He guides us because his reputation is at stake—*for His name's sake*. As the Lord's sheep we can count on his guiding us in the right way in life, because his name or reputation as a faithful shepherd is on the line. He will not let us wander without his faithful intervention. The Apostle Paul implied this when he wrote, *For all who are being led by the Spirit of God, these are the sons of God* (Rom. 8:14).

The Lord is also our shepherd **in the seasons of life** (vv. 4-5). Verse 4 describes what we might call a "season of shadows." *Even though I walk through the valley of the shadow of death, I fear no evil, for You are with me; Your rod and Your staff, they comfort me.* A shepherd may lead his flock unexpectedly through a valley or ravine in the Palestinian wilderness. Or, as some have suggested, he may find it necessary to lead the flock through such a ravine to get to better pasture at a higher elevation.[33] Such valleys could be dangerous. There was the possibility of flash floods, as well as the presence of dangerous predators; but the shepherd would guide and guard his flock with his rod (to ward off predators) and staff (to rescue them when in trouble).

So, the Lord may lead us also through difficult passages in life. When He does, we may wonder if we have lost our way; and it's possible when we encounter such valleys that we have wandered from his way. However, it's not necessarily the case, for we know that God does guide us through difficult seasons of life. Jesus said, *In the world you have tribulation* (John 16:33). The apostle Paul said, *Through many tribulations we must enter the kingdom of God* (Acts 14:22b). Though we may be surprised at the valleys we encounter in life, we need not be overcome by fear of them. When I looked at this psalm on Polly's wall, this is what it was telling us; that though we may encounter evil in this life, we may gain confidence in the face of it because God is with us. The implication is that He is greater than any evil we may face.

I have often heard people say that God will not allow us to experience anything He knows we can't handle. I don't believe it for a minute. Paul said that when he and his companions were in Asia, they *were burdened excessively, beyond* their *strength* (II Cor. 1:8). God does allow us to bear burdens greater than *our* capacity to bear—but they are not beyond *his* ability to help us bear. That is what this psalm assures us of—that no evil is ultimately beyond the Lord—and the Lord is with us.

This is likely one of the reasons He may lead us or allow us to navigate such valleys in life, and it is hinted at in this section by the way in which the psalmist refers to the Lord. You will notice that in the first three verses, he speaks of the Lord in the third person: *He* and *his*.

Beginning in verse 4, however, he speaks of the Lord in the second person: *You* and *your*. He is not just speaking *about* the Lord, but *to* the Lord—and there's no question as to which is more personal. *He* is "shoulder to shoulder." *You* is "face to face." Perhaps the psalmist is telling us that it is in the valley that we may come to know and appreciate the Lord as in no other context of life.[34] If we were to survey the readers of this book and ask when it was that they came to know the Lord more intimately, it's very likely that the vast majority would acknowledge that it was during a difficult season of life—during a season of shadows.

One of my loves in life is the study of theology. Over the years I've sat in more theology classes than I can remember. I came to know a lot *about* God in theology class. Yet I can honestly say that I learned to *know* God, not in theology class, but in the nursing home at the side of Polly's bed. There is a difference—a great difference, between knowing a lot *about* God and *knowing* God. If nothing more comes out of our time spent in the valley other than that we came to know God in a much deeper way, this alone would make it worth all the trouble we endured.

Notice, however, that the valley is not a destination. God leads us *through* the valley. It may be that verse 5 describes the outcome of being led by God through such an experience. It describes a "season of blessing." *You prepare a table before me in the presence of my enemies; You have anointed my head with oil; My cup overflows.* Many commentators suggest that here David transitions from using the imagery of the shepherd to that of a gracious host in this verse.[35] Perhaps the image of a shepherd could not exhaust all that the Lord had meant to David in life. Or, perhaps in this verse David is simply picturing the shepherd as a host to his flock.[36] It really doesn't matter. What does matter is that here he paints a picture of the Lord graciously providing a bounteous meal, perhaps a thanksgiving feast for his deliverances in the valley. The fact that enemies are noted as being close at hand implies that previously they may have posed a threat—but no longer. They have been overcome and are being held back by the Lord. It was the host's responsibility to provide fragrant oil to anoint and refresh his guests; and that is what He does here. As for his cup—it's full to the brim—overflowing in fact. It's a picture of generosity and abundant provision. Our entrance into the final phase of our salvation, into God's eternal kingdom, is often pictured as sitting down to feast with the Lord and his people.[37] Yet even during this life there are times when God mercifully grants us small foretastes of this ultimate feast. They are "seasons of blessing."

When we are in the valley, it's tempting for us to flee—to trade the narrow path for what we think will be greener pastures. When we do, however, we forfeit the blessings described here. We also miss out on the opportunity of coming to know the Lord in a deeper way, to learn of Him in ways only possible in the valley. Even so, our faithful shepherd will come after us to restore us to his righteous path.[38]

The Lord is our shepherd in the daily rhythm of life, in the seasons of life. Now He is our shepherd *for the rest of our life* (v. 6).

Surely goodness and lovingkindness will follow me all the days of my life, And I will dwell in the house of the Lord forever (lit. "for length of days"). Having reflected on what the Lord has meant to him, and still does, David expresses a confident assurance that the *goodness* and *lovingkindness* which the Lord had shown him in the past would continue to pursue him to the end of his days. Might there be another valley ahead? Perhaps. Even a valley that might last the rest of our life. Yet there would not be one day in which God's mercies would not also be present. In the psychiatric hospital where I have served as chaplain for many years, there is a unit devoted to patients being treated for various addictions. Years ago there were two signs posted over the exit doors in this unit. One read, "By the grace of God." The other read, "One day at a time." What a wonderful reminder these signs were to all of us who passed through this unit.

It's possible that when David wrote this psalm he was for some reason unable to enjoy the presence of the Lord. Perhaps he was physically distanced from the sanctuary, the place of worship and fellowship with God. He was confident, though, that it would not always be so; and he desired nothing more than to be restored to such fellowship. I think it's not too much to say that his hope of being restored to the *house of the Lord* on earth is a picture of our hope of entering into our eternal home. One day we too will enter into eternal fellowship with Him. We shall forever be with the Lord. Until then, however, the Lord is with us and promises not to leave or forsake us.

The words of this wonderful psalm, imprinted on the poster on Polly's wall, were a daily reminder of our Lord's shepherding care—and they encouraged us as nothing else quite could.

Chapter XI

INCREASING CHALLENGES

I mentioned in a previous chapter that I had begun serving as chaplain at a local hospital in the Dallas area (actually two hospitals). "How did this happen?" you might be thinking. Good question. When I began serving at Probe Ministries, I had no idea how long I might be serving there. I began with the intention of remaining as long as I believed I was being useful in this ministry, which for all I knew might have been for the rest of my life. The years spent there were fruitful years in my estimation. After a few years, however, I realized that if I was going to remain effective in this ministry, I was going to have to travel from time to time, to participate in the various conferences that Probe conducted. At least, this is how it appeared to me. With Polly's declining condition, I did not see how I could in good conscience do this. Even though she was in good care at the nursing home, her needs were great and I was not willing to leave her solely in the care of the nursing home staff for very long. Many days I went to see her twice, once over the noon hour and then again at night. I at times wondered how I was going to be able to continue in ministry at all, and take care of Polly, as well as raise our two growing children.

One day I was having lunch with a friend who had recently resigned from his pastorate. In the course of our conversation I asked him what he was hoping to do now. He rattled off a list of options he felt were before him—including "hospital chaplaincy." I don't know why this stuck in my mind, but it did. It seemed that over the next several weeks, God brought this ministry to my attention on a number of occasions. I will be honest that hospital chaplaincy is not something I had ever had any interest in pursuing. It wasn't even on my "long list" of ministries to consider. Yet over and over again it seemed like God was drawing it to my attention. I prayed about whether this might be what the Lord would have me to do and I investigated what might be involved in taking steps toward this end.

I had a friend who had been serving as chaplain at a large hospital nearby for a number of years, Brian Quinn. Brian had been a student of mine at the seminary when I was teaching there. In fact, he told me that it was through a guest lecturer in a class I taught at the seminary on pastoral ministry that he was directed toward hospital work. I decided to ask if I could spend part of a day with him, just to see what this kind of work would be like. He was more than willing to help. I'll be honest, that after spending half a day with him in the hospital, I came away feeling that this was just too intense. I couldn't imagine being around so much crisis and trauma all day long and then returning home to take care of my wife and children in the evenings. So I left feeling that this was something I would definitely not want to do. God, however, apparently had other plans. Over the next several weeks, it seemed that He drew my attention to hospital ministry at every turn. So I decided to take steps to see what would be entailed in beginning to serve in the hospital.

Brian directed me to Dr. Doug Cecil, the Alumni Director at Dallas Seminary, who had contacts in some smaller local hospitals. I had known Doug as well from his student days at the seminary while I was teaching there. Doug has a huge heart and he was more than anxious to help. He directed me to the ministry of Hospital Chaplains' Ministry of America (now Healthcare Chaplains Ministry Association), an evangelical agency that trains and certifies healthcare chaplains. He also opened the door for me to begin serving as full time volunteer chaplain at a nearby community hospital, where I began in December of 1996. Little did I realize how God had been preparing me for this ministry through all the years of caregiving—but He indeed had.

Hospital chaplaincy is a challenging and rewarding ministry. As is true in most types of work or ministry, there are phases through which one passes in the course of carrying out this kind of work. I found that there were many adjustments to be made during the early years in the hospital. Being around illness, crisis and trauma every day can be very exhilarating, even if at times very stressful. Yet after several years of being exposed to the kinds of things that happen in a hospital every day, what was once new and exciting can become familiar and routine. As a result, a chaplain can find him or herself simply "going through the motions" of ministry. It's at this point that I found myself asking, "Am I really and truly here for these people and for the Lord—not just in body but in heart and soul?" Over time I learned that it's through the daily disciplines of prayer and meditating on God's Word that our hearts are renewed and prepared for the opportunities for ministry that may lie hidden beneath the ordinary encounters of everyday life in the hospital.

Then, after so many years in this kind of work, it's easy to grow weary and tired. When this happens, though this may be God's way of redirecting us to another avenue of ministry, it may also simply be time to recognize that God has given us the privilege of serving here for many years, and He wants us to train and equip others to minister in these ways as well. He may also have other ministries that He wants us to engage in alongside our work in the hospitals. It's time to renew our commitment to serving the Lord where He has planted us—one day at a time, for the long haul.

The transition to hospital ministry was also occasioned by another change in our family's life. A few years before, my mother had been diagnosed with Alzheimer's disease.[39] My mother was a very gifted person. She had a wonderful singing voice and had taught piano many years of her life. She also had served as teacher, and later principal in a Christian school in California. In the early 1990s, however, it gradually became evident that her memory and her mind were becoming unraveled. She and my father had retired to the Seattle area at the time and it was a matter of great concern to us what was happening to them.

A year or two after Polly entered the nursing home, my folks moved to our area to be closer to us. For several years my dad cared for my mom at home. Bless his heart, he did the very best he could. In fact, due to his conscientious nature, he attempted to do far more than anyone reasonably could.

At times, Mom provided us with some rather humorous experiences — such as the time she was with us at a restaurant and she looked at the large lemon slice floating in her water and suddenly plucked it out and swallowed it whole. She then gave us the biggest smile and just laughed. We couldn't help but laugh with her.

On occasion, she would say the most endearing things as well. When she was being examined by her doctor, his nurse asked her a series of questions to test her memory. Mom was evidently frustrated by this battery of questions, and she finally said to her, "I used to remember all those things, but now all I know is that I'm a little girl who is loved by Jesus."

Sometimes, however, the effects of her illness on her behavior made things extremely difficult to manage. As a result, there were often reasons for us to be seriously concerned for my dad's safety and wellbeing.

Approximately a year after moving to our area, it became necessary for us to seek nursing home placement for my mother, as her care had grown far beyond my dad's ability to manage. The Lord led us to a wonderful Alzheimer's care unit at the Mary Trew Home, run by the Southern Baptists in Dallas. What a special place this was—and especially for my parents.

Though it took a few weeks for my mom to adjust to being in the special care unit which became her home, she eventually grew very comfortable there. She was safe; and so was my dad. Though the staff advised him to visit only rarely, he resolved to see her every day. I think this was a good thing.

The staff was wonderful in caring for her and the other residents. One of the things my mother enjoyed very much was the sing-alongs. It was amazing to me that though Mom could remember very little, and could hardly put together a coherent sentence, singing was altogether different. She could sing an entire song from memory. There's something about words set to music that apparently frees the brain and mind of at least some of its limitations.

I often would go to see my mom over the noon hour, and would sit in the small dining room with her and the other residents, to eat lunch with her at her table. Sometimes she would decline the meal, saying she wasn't hungry, but I would go ahead and start eating the lunch they served me. After a couple minutes, she would start snacking off my plate. So I would ask her, "Are you hungry after all?" She would smile sheepishly and say, "Yes," and they would bring her a lunch plate of her own.

Not many months after my mom entered the special care unit, things started to unravel in my dad's life as well. It began a couple weeks after I was in an auto wreck, coming off a freeway onto an exit near our home. Though I hardly remember approaching the intersection at the end of the exit, I do vividly remember the loud crashing sound and the sight of the front end of another vehicle bearing down on me from my left, just inches from my face. The fact that I survived with only fractured ribs was a near miracle. Fractured ribs are very painful. Every time I sneezed or coughed or laughed, every time I had to stand up from lying down, it was like a knife was being thrust in my side. When I was at the hospital the night of the accident, the nurse who transferred me from the ER to my room thought he would ease my discomfort by cracking jokes.

Every joke, however, made me feel like my ribs were cracking all over again. At least I was laughing and breathing. It could easily have been a lot worse.

A couple weeks after this event, I took my dad to a high school basketball game as a break from the routine of caregiving. At the half time, he walked down to the concession area to purchase a snack. When he came back he told me that he felt strange. He said, "Rick, when I spoke to the person tending the concession, I ordered something completely different from what I had planned to ask for. Something is happening to my mind." I had no idea.

A day or two later, Dad's thinking started becoming quite bizarre. He began telling me the strangest things I had ever heard, including his belief that the world was coming to an end—and it was his fault. This was just the beginning of the most unusual experience I have ever had with any friend or loved one. I had never seen anyone acting or thinking like Dad was. For the next two weeks I couldn't even leave him alone.

It was difficult to see him like this. Dad was a humble and warm-hearted man, who had devoted his life to ministry. For many years he had sustained a personal ministry to professional athletes. One of the joys of growing up in our family was meeting some of these sports figures who occasionally visited us in our home in the San Francisco area—players like Felipe Alou, Orlando Cepeda, and Jose Pagan. For some reason, however, he had fallen into what I later realized was a seriously psychotic condition. He was hearing and imagining things that were entirely unreal.

I finally realized that Dad needed the help of a psychiatrist and I encouraged him to go with me to be evaluated. At first, this was absolutely out of the question for him. So I called my brother Paul in Detroit and asked him to come down to be with us. I was so glad he came. Together, we encouraged Dad to see a Christian psychiatrist and after a number of long discussions, he agreed.

What we learned was that due to the years of unremitting stress of caring for my mom, topped off by the near fatal accident I had recently been in, Dad's constitution had been weakened to the point that his thinking had become very irrational. Reflecting back on those days moves me almost to tears for him. He found himself in this condition, not because of anything wrong he had done, but because he had tried so hard to do what he believed was right—caring for his wife and family. In fact, he really tried to do the humanly impossible. I have seen other caregivers attempt to do the same.

Dad's doctor put him on some medication that he felt would help him over the course of several weeks. However, as the weeks, and then months went by, Dad made hardly any progress. He lost at least 50 pounds. When I visited him in his room, I would find him staring at the ceiling, with an expressionless look on his face. I was frankly concerned that if he went on like this for very long, he would not survive.

For several months, I had responsibility of caring for three family members who were in healthcare institutions: Polly, my mom, and now my dad who was pretty much confined to his room in the assisted care section of the Mary Trew Home. I tried to see each of them once every day. I remember telling myself that it couldn't be this way forever. I found myself simply asking God for the wisdom and strength to know what to do that particular day. That's all I knew to do. He did answer that prayer, a day at a time.

Finally, after nearly six months with very little evidence of improvement, it was suggested that Dad consider taking ECT (electro-convulsive therapy), or what is popularly called "shock treatment." I had never known anyone personally who had received this treatment, but I felt this was the only option we had. Mind you, we were praying and asking others to pray as well. After this treatment was suggested, I "randomly" encountered three other people who had been amazingly helped by ECT. I felt this was providential.

Dad ultimately had ECT, administered while he was an inpatient in the psychiatric unit of the Zale Lipshy Hospital in Dallas. Normally, this treatment entails three treatments a week, for three to five weeks, which he had. Amazingly, however, after the very first treatment he experienced a dramatic reversal of his condition. He did not even remember the terribly bizarre things that had occurred the previous six months. I think even his doctor was amazed. I believe it was an answer to prayer. My recounting my father's experience with ECT is not intended as a blanket endorsement of ECT for all seriously depressed people. I do believe, however, that this was God's provision for him at this time in his life.

Sometimes God answers prayer apart from any means at all. In such cases, God's power is clearly made visible. Most times, however, it seems God includes the use of normal means in answering our prayers, for reasons known only to Him. In such cases, it's God's wisdom rather than his power that is more clearly in focus. His wisdom is made known through his ability to orchestrate the ordinary means of grace in applying them to our afflictions.

God could have healed Timothy of his stomach ailments directly, apart from any means; and Paul could have urged him to simply pray for such healing—but he didn't. Instead, he told him to take some medicinal wine for his stomach (I Tim. 5:23). God could have cured Dad apart from any means, but He chose to do it by means of ECT.

Dad's condition dramatically improved during the second half of 1997. He was able to buy a house and move into it with me at the end of that summer. Over the following years he resumed a fairly normal life. My mother's condition, however, dramatically worsened; and she was hospitalized in early December for pneumonia, in the very hospital where I was training for chaplaincy.

Friday evening, December 12, 1997, I was driving in my car and listening to a Christian radio station. They were broadcasting the program produced by Probe Ministries that evening; and they happened to be airing one of a series of programs that I had opportunity to write for them a few years prior, on the subject of "Heaven." I was thankful to hear this at this time. The next morning, at 7:30am, the phone rang at our home. It was my mom's nurse at the hospital telling us that she had departed for heaven just moments before.

When I told Polly that my mom had passed away, she seemed to have tears in her eyes as she said to me in her barely audible voice, "She's singing now." My mom loved to sing and had a wonderful voice. I can only imagine that the addition of her voice did not go unnoticed in the heavenly choir.

Shortly after my mom passed away, someone sent us this poem. It seems to reflect what she would probably want us to hear.

Christmas in Heaven

I've had my first Christmas in Heaven;

Oh glorious, wonderful day!

I stood with the saints of the ages,

Who found Christ the Truth and the Way.

I sang with the heavenly choir;

Just think! I, who longed so to sing!

And Oh, what celestial music

We brought to our Savior and King!

We sang the glad songs of redemption,

How Jesus to Bethlehem came,

And how they called His name Jesus,

That all might be saved through His name.

We sang once again with the angels,

The song that they sang that blest morn,

When shepherds first heard the glad story

That Jesus, the Savior, was born.

Oh Darling, I wish you had been here;

No Christmas on earth could compare

With all the rapture and glory

We witnessed in Heaven so fair.

You know how I always loved Christmas;

It seemed such a wonderful day,

With all of my loved ones around me,

The children so happy at play.

Yes, now I can see why I loved it;

And, oh, what a joy it will be

When you and my loved ones are with me,

To share in the glories I see.

So dear ones on earth, here's my greeting:

Look up 'till the Day Star appears,

And Oh, what a Christmas awaits us,

Beyond all our partings and tears!

By A. S. Reitz[40]

Dad survived Mom by another fifteen years. In his later years, he was cared for by my dear brother Paul and his family in southern California, residing in a group home the last few years of his life before going home to be with the Lord, November 13, 2012.

At the end of 1997, my mother was in heaven and my dad was much better—but Polly was still in her nursing home, and she still had many "miles" to go in her journey.

Chapter XII

A LONG OBEDIENCE [41]

I had prayed for Polly's healing many times, for many years. As time went by, however, it became evident to me (much as it did to the Apostle Paul as he records in II Corinthians 12:8-9) that God's purpose was not for the healing of Polly's body this side of heaven. He had something else in mind.

Not that I was unconvinced of God's ability to heal. In fact, serving as chaplain in a hospital for so many years, I've witnessed not a few remarkable recoveries, including at least one that I believe was a genuine miracle. I was walking down a hall at the hospital one afternoon, when I heard a man weeping loudly in his room. When I entered, I saw a fellow sitting on his bed crying. I asked him what the problem was. He said, "It's my sin. It's my sin."

This man was in the hospital for a very serious illness. I could tell even by his appearance. He told me that his doctor had informed him that he couldn't do anything more for him and he was sending him to a larger hospital to see if there was something they might do for him. At the moment, however, he was focused only on his sin.

"There's a remedy for that, you know," I said to him. He said, "I know." For the next several minutes we talked about his sin, and the need for repentance and God's grace. At the end of our conversation, he prayed what seemed to me a genuine prayer of repentance. I left, assuring him of my prayers.

The next morning I returned to this man's room, to see how he was doing. When I knocked on his door I found him packing up his clothes to leave. "Where are you going?" I asked him. He said, "I'm going home. The doctor told me I'm well and I don't need any treatment." I could tell just by looking at him that what he said was true. What a change from the day before.

After wishing him well, I walked over to the nurses' station for that unit and saw this man's doctor standing there writing in his chart. "What happened to this patient?" I asked him. He looked at me and said, "He's well. I've never seen anything like it and I have no way to explain it. I'm sending him home."

I really believe God gave this man a second chance at life. The interesting thing to me is that in our prayer, we didn't even pray for his physical healing. We prayed for his spiritual healing—for the forgiveness of his confessed sins. It very well may be that this man's illness was in some way connected to his sin; and when he dealt with his sin, God removed his illness. James says concerning the sick person, *(A)nd if he has committed sins, they will be forgiven him. Therefore, confess your sins to one another, and pray for one another so that you may be healed* (James 5:15b-16a). Though sickness is part of the consequence of our living in a world staggering under the weight of mankind's sin, not all sickness is due to one's personal sin.[42] Some sickness, however, is; and when this is the case, genuine repentance and prayer can result not only in spiritual, but physical healing as well.[43] It seemed to me this was such a case.

However, with many people, this is not the case; and I believe it is not always God's purpose to bring physical healing in this life. John Wimber himself said that when it comes to healing, "God has the sovereign choice concerning each person for whom we pray. Will he heal, or will he extend grace for suffering instead?"[44]

I remember entering the room of another patient at the hospital one day. The patient was a young woman with a serious illness. A middle age female friend was with her, who said to me, "We've been claiming healing and rebuking demons all day, and she's not getting any better. I don't know if the problem is her sin, or my lack of faith. Can you help us?" Well, if the only cause of a Christian's being ill is either their sin or lack of faith, this leaves a lot of people believing that the only reason for their illness is their own spiritual deficiency. I don't believe that the evidence of Scripture supports this conclusion.

There are many people in the Bible described as experiencing illness, with no indication that the reason was their spiritual deficiency. Some were healed. Others were not. Sarah suffered from infertility until God miraculously reversed her condition. Isaac suffered blindness in his old age (Gen. 27:1). Jacob suffered a hip injury from which he apparently never fully recovered (Gen. 32:25). He also suffered an illness which eventually proved fatal (Gen. 48:1; 49:33). Mephibosheth was lame in his feet, due to being dropped as a child (II Sam. 9:3). The prophet Ahijah was blind in his old age (I Kings 13:14). Job suffered severe physical affliction and many tragedies. Paul suffered a "thorn in the flesh"

(II Cor. 12:7-10), which may have been an eye ailment (Gal. 4:13-15). Paul's friend Epaphroditus was ill almost to the point of death, though he recovered (Phil. 2:25-30). Timothy suffered *frequent ailments* (I Tim. 5:23). Trophimus *was left sick at Miletus* by Paul (II Tim. 4:20).

Of particular interest is the fact that the Apostle Paul's physical ailment (though intended by Satan as an obstacle to his ministry) was intended by God to keep him from spiritual ruin. It was more important to God that Paul be kept from sinful pride, than that he be kept in perfect physical health (II Cor. 12:7-10). Though God is certainly able to bring healing, and sometimes does, there are times when his purposes entail his allowing illness to remain. This was obviously true in Polly's case, as it is in the case of many others who suffer lifelong afflictions.[45]

About four years after Polly's initially entering the nursing home, I was able to move her to a brand new home, a bit closer to where we lived, and situated on Lake Ray Hubbard, some miles east of Dallas. Polly had a view of the lake out her window. This would prove to be even more of a blessing than I realized at the time.

I had continued to bring Polly on regular outings. One Saturday afternoon I brought her to a beautiful Greek Orthodox Church in our area to see some of the art work in their sanctuary. Due to her weakness, however, I realized it was going to be impossible for me to get her inside. I slowly put her back in the car, and drove her back to the nursing home. On the way back, I said to myself, "This is probably the last time Polly will ever be able to go out with me." It was.

For the last five or so years of her life, she was never removed from her bed except to be taken for a bath, or to the hospital. No longer was it a matter of bringing her to places she could enjoy, but it was a matter of bringing some joy to her bedside.

One of the things I had enjoyed doing in years past was bringing Polly on rides through neighborhoods that were color-fully decorated with lights during the Christmas season. She used to love going on these rides. She no longer could. So my daughter and I decided to take our video camera along and record as much as we could of our tour past these beautifully lit homes in Dallas. What we were able to show Polly was a very poor substitute for the real thing, but it was better than nothing.

In January of 2000 it was discovered that Polly had a large lump in her breast. I made an appointment with an oncologist at Baylor University Medical Center in Dallas, and it was determined that she indeed had breast cancer. Surgery was scheduled in February for a radical mastectomy. Following her surgery, she was put on tamoxifin, a drug commonly used to treat women who have had breast cancer. I asked her oncologist if he suggested anything more aggressive. He said that particularly in light of her overall condition, he did not.

Polly's life was becoming increasingly confined. She had been bedfast for a few years now and the highlight of each day was simply getting a bath. Actually, in the nursing home, they only bathe the residents three times a week. When someone is lying in bed twenty-four hours a day, it's important to keep their skin as clean as possible. So for several years I had made it my practice to bathe her on the days that the nursing home did not, lifting her onto a special chair that I could wheel down to the shower room. I was especially alert to signs of damage to her skin, as this could result in a life threatening infection. I knew every inch of her body. My greatest joy was simply knowing that she was clean and as comfortable as possible. Sometimes I would go to see her over my lunch hour, to wash her face and brush her teeth and place a few drops of juice on her tongue just for the taste. Sometimes, massaging her calves and feet, or her arms and hands, was the best thing I could do for her. Though she could not speak, her wonderful smile was all I needed to see. It was my greatest reward.

It had been my custom to spend an hour or two with her each evening. It was a quiet time in the nursing home. This particular nursing home had 137 beds and it was full. Yet there were just two of us (myself and the daughter of an elderly female resident) who were there every night.

At the end of my nightly visits, I always made sure she was comfortable and secure for the night. I usually left her radio quietly playing Christian music, or even a baseball game by her bed, and asked her nurse to turn it off when Polly was asleep. Shutting off her light, I walked to the doorway and looked back to see her following me with her eyes. Turning to walk down the hall and out to the dimly lit parking lot for the fifteen minute drive home in the quiet darkness was the hardest thing I did every day.

We had read from the Scriptures every day since she first entered the nursing home in 1992, but we began reading more about heaven now. One book that I read for Polly was Joni

Eareckson Tada's book, *Heaven: Your Real Home*.[46] I could tell that Polly was listening intently. Listening to worshipful music was also a source of comfort and encouragement, now more than ever. In years past I had taken her to many Christian concerts in our area, but now I could at least play the CDs of many Christian artists. I recall our listening to a song that included lyrics describing our heavenly destination, where we will be finally free of this life's trials. I wondered if Polly was listening. A tear silently streaming down her cheek told me that she was.

One evening a few years before, while reading through the first chapter of Paul's letter to the Philippians, I noticed Polly was dosing off to sleep—or so it seemed. When I came to the section of the chapter, however, in which Paul writes that to be with Christ is "better by far," she opened her eyes and lifted up her head and with a big smile on her face, she said in her then slurred speech, "I know that." She then closed her eyes and resumed her restful pose.

As Polly's life became more and more narrow and confined, I at times found myself questioning the value of living such a restricted life—both for her, and for me as her caregiver. I realized that Polly could linger for a number of years in her silent and solitary life. I remember driving on the freeway to her nursing home one day, and saying, "Lord, I don't understand the reason for our life right now—but if you decide that the best way we can bring glory to you is by our living out the remainder of our days like this, I'm willing. If this means spending the rest of my life at her bedside, until You take her home, then give us the grace to do it one day at a time."

People sometimes ask if I ever considered leaving Polly. I can tell you that I never did. I did not know why God had allowed all of this to happen to us, but I did know that abandoning her was not the way to deal with it. How could I leave her in her time of need? I would never do it. I am so thankful that the Lord gave me the wisdom and grace to remain by her side. I would never want her to, but if she had to walk through this valley a second time, I can honestly say that I would be first in line to walk through it with her again.

Though I'm well aware that there are occasions when a marriage may suffer a mortal wound, Christian marriage is a sacred bond. The Apostle Paul likens marriage to the relationship between Christ and his church. This is an exalted view of marriage. It tells us that marriage is far more than a relationship in which two people seek to satisfy their own needs or desires from one another.

It tells us that it can be the platform in which God demonstrates something of his own faithful love for us through our mutual relationship. Marriage can be the context in which God can use each of us as a catalyst for our mutual spiritual growth, teaching us to love someone who is different than ourselves—not just during the good times, but during the tough times as well. Someone has pointed out that if all it took for marriage to succeed was for us to do "what comes naturally," it wouldn't be necessary to consecrate marriage with a vow, because marriage will require of us what does *not* come naturally[47] Though I do not believe that God calls us to passively tolerate behavior that is selfish and abusive, I do know that marriage will require us to serve the best interest of the one we've been called to love—sometimes at sacrifice to ourself. This means that marriage will require faith—faith that God will give us all we need, not only to remain faithful to our vows, but to use our marriage to shape our lives to be more like his. I was learning that God is more than adequate, not only to help us withstand the storms of life, but to use those storms to strengthen our faith in Him and to deepen our love for each other. I can tell you that in our case, God proved worthy of our trust.

How much longer Polly would linger I could not know, but I was prepared for it to be longer than shorter. I can also tell you that the longer her journey lasted, one of the things I thanked the Lord for was the care she received every day from her physicians and the nursing home staff. They were gifts of God's grace.

Chapter XIII

SHOULD A CHRISTIAN USE A PHYSICIAN? [48]

—⸺⸺—

T his may sound like a strange question to most of us. From time to time, however, I encounter patients in the hospitals for whom seeking the help of a medical doctor poses a crisis of faith. As I related earlier, there were a couple times when it was suggested to us that our relying on the help of physicians portrayed a lack of faith in God.

There is no question that God has the power to bring healing in a miraculous way, without the use of any means other than prayer. We are instructed when we are suffering affliction of any kind that we are to bring our needs to God in prayer (James 5:13). Prayer is not something we resort to "when all else fails." It's our first resort, everywhere and always. This does not imply, however, that it is always God's purpose to respond to our prayers apart from the use of what we might consider the "ordinary means of grace." Many have observed that while God-fearing farmers certainly pray for a good harvest, they do not neglect to plow their fields, and plant and water their seed.[49] Likewise, I believe Scripture teaches that medical science (as well as other health promoting practices) is one of God's "ordinary means of grace." It's one of the means God has provided to alleviate some of the effects of humanity's fall into sin.

When God gave his law to the nation Israel through Moses, He included measures that would prevent illness and promote health among his people. For example, though there were certainly other reasons for many of the dietary restrictions in Israel's law, some of them no doubt protected Israel from exposure to disease (Lev. 11:1-47). Even though there were spiritual lessons to be learned from their laws, practices such as the quarantine of people with infectious skin diseases (Lev. 13:1-14:57; Num. 5:4), sterilization (Lev. 11:32, 39-40; Num. 19:11; 31:22-23) as well as laws relating to public sanitation (Ex. 29:14; Dt. 23:12-14) also promoted Israel's physical wellbeing. Likewise, we should not ignore health promoting practices such as these and expect that God will preserve us from the natural results.

Though what we think of as the practice of medicine was far less sophisticated than what we have today, nonetheless there were physicians in biblical times, in Israel as well as in other nations. The physician-priests of other nations relied on natural remedies of various kinds, but also on magic and incantations. Israel was forbidden from resorting to these pagan practices. This does not mean, however, that there was no place for the legitimate practice of medicine as it was understood in biblical times. From earliest times, the priests played a role in discerning the health condition of people in Israel. In time, there were also others who special-ized in the practice of medicine. The rabbinic writings record the presence of a physician at the temple in Jerusalem to care for the priests (Mishnah, *Shekalim*, v. 1). There were also physicians in each city (Babylonian Talmud, Gittin, 12b), licensed by the city authorities (Babylonian Talmud, Baba Bathra, 21a).[50]

Though people in Old Testament times were exhorted to go first to the priest in time of illness (Lev. 13), physicians and the use of medical practices known at that time are spoken of in a favorable light in a number of biblical passages. Isaiah speaks of treating wounds with bandage and oil (1:6). Jeremiah speaks of the healing properties of the *balm in Gilead* and the proper work of the physician (8:22). He also speaks of the cleansing properties of soap (2:22). God brought healing to King Hezekiah in part through the application of a fig poultice on a boil (II Kings 20:7-8). Job found some relief by draining the toxins from his sores (2:8). It's true that King Asa was reprimanded for resorting to physicians (II Chron. 16:11-14). However, these were certainly physicians who resorted to pagan practices. His sin was in failing to turn to the Lord, not in seeking the help of legitimate physicians.

The intertestamental Jewish writer Ben Sira wrote of the blessings of physicians and of their work as the gift of God. "Show the physician due honor in view of your need of him, for the Lord has created him; healing comes from the Most High.... The Lord has created medicines out of the earth, and a sensible man will not refuse them.... And he has given men knowledge so that he might be glorified for his wonderful works. With them he cures and takes away pain, the druggist makes a mixture of them.... (L)eave room for the physician, for the Lord has created him, and he must not desert you, for you need him. There is a time when your welfare depends upon them, for they too will pray the Lord to guide them to bringing relief and effecting a cure and restoration to health."[51] Though this passage is not a part of inspired Scripture, it does reflect the beliefs of a God-fearing Jewish writer of that time.

In the New Testament, Jesus recognized the legitimate role of physicians and medicine when he said, *Those who are well have no need of a physician, but those who are sick* (Mt. 9:12). Jesus' likening his own redemptive mission to that of a physician would hardly be likely if He did not see their work as legitimate and beneficial. In the parable about the Good Samaritan, Jesus spoke approvingly of the use of typical medical treatments of his day (Lk. 10:34). Paul referred to Luke as the *beloved physician* (Col. 4:14), and he encouraged Timothy to make use of wine as a medicinal treatment for his stomach ailments (I Tim. 5:23). The woman who had suffered a hemorrhage for twelve years was said to have *endured much at the hands of many physicians, and had spent all that she had and was not helped at all* (Mk. 5:25-26). This certainly emphasizes the intractable nature of her ailment, and the obvious limitations of physicians in this case. It also highlights the miraculous nature of her cure through the power of Jesus. However, in light of the other Scriptures we have noted, it is by no means a blanket indictment of the medical profession.

In light of these things, I think it's more than fair to say that the work of properly trained physicians is a gift from God. It is part of his common grace to humanity, in bringing some measure of relief from the curse of illness. Certainly, God can intervene in a special and supernatural way when called for by his purposes— and there are occasions when He certainly does. Nevertheless, we should not limit Him to working only in this extraordinary way. In praying with patients in the hospital, I make it a general practice to thank God for the resources and skills He has entrusted to the medical staff, as well as for the healing properties He has created in our own bodies. Though we pray that God might work even beyond what He can accomplish through these means, in keeping with his will, we certainly do not minimize these wonderful provisions of his grace. I am certainly thankful to God for the help that Polly received through several competent and compassionate physicians and other members of the health care community, to the very last day of her life.

Chapter XIV

FINAL DAYS

E arly on the morning of July 24, 2003, I was up and getting ready for the day. As I was shaving and brushing my teeth, a Christian radio station was playing in the background. I walked across my room to sit down on my bed and read the day's selection from "Our Daily Bread" (the devotional from RBC Ministries).[52] As I reached over to turn off the radio, I heard this comment by the spokesperson: "What would you say if you knew tomorrow would be the last day of your loved one's life?" An interesting comment. I sat down and opened the devotional. The title for that day was "Say It Now!" Here is part of the text of that day's devotion.

"An unknown author has penned these thought-provoking words:

I would rather have one little rose

From the garden of a friend

Than to have the choicest flowers

When my stay on earth must end.

I would rather have a pleasant word

In kindness said to me

Than flattery when my heart is still,

And life has ceased to be.

I would rather have a loving smile

From friends I know are true

Than tears shed 'round my casket

When to this world I bid adieu....

Recalling the good qualities of deceased friends or relatives at their funeral is appropriate, but how much better to give sincere praise to them while they are still living. It may be the encouragement they desperately need.

Do you owe someone a word of thanks or appreciation? Don't put it off. Say it today. Tomorrow may be too late! — Richard De Haan"[53]

I don't need to tell you that these words captured my attention, particularly coming right after the comment I had heard on the radio just a moment before. It was more than coincidental. I wasn't sure how to receive these words, but as I went through my day, I resolved to tell Polly that evening how much I loved her.

As usual, I went to the nursing home that night. While I was there, a lady came by Polly's room with some flowers. She was a personal acquaintance, but this was the first (and only) time she visited. I gave Polly a bath that evening. As I prepared to wheel her back to her room, I stooped down to her eye level and said to her, "Polly, I just want you to know how much I love you and I want to thank you for all that you did for me and the kids during the years you were at home with us. We are so grateful for you. You have been an example to us through the years; and I want you to know that there are hundreds of people, all over the world, who know about your life and are praying for you."

Polly had been unable to speak at all for quite some time now, but the look in her dark brown eyes, as she stared directly at me, spoke more than any words could say.

At my usual time, I left to return home for the night.

It was the next evening that I received the call from Polly's nurse asking me to meet her at the hospital's ER. I pulled into the parking lot and walked toward the ER entrance. The staff greeted me and showed me where Polly was. As I remember, she was barely conscious, as they gave her oxygen and breathing treatment. Late that Friday night, they sent her to a room on the third floor.

This was not the first time Polly had experienced pneumonia, but it was definitely the hardest. The next two weeks were a struggle, as they administered antibiotics and breathing treatments. I did my best to make her comfortable. Thankfully, she was able to sleep soundly at night.

On August 5, over the noon hour, I stopped by her room to see how she was doing. She did not look well. I had to go on to the psych hospital where I served part time as chaplain, but I told her nurse I would be back as soon as possible.

On my way to the psych hospital, I received a page again. It was her nurse telling me that Polly had gone into respiratory distress. I turned around and headed back to Polly's hospital. When I arrived, they were giving her morphine. She soon fell into a deep sleep.

Her doctor came by the room. I asked him, "Doctor, what reasonable measures can we take to help Polly now?" He said to me, "Well, I could put her on a respirator, but she's so weak she would never come off it." I knew that Polly would not want to live in that condition, with no hope of recovery. As a hospital chaplain I had seen families insist on heroic measures for their loved one, only to prolong and add pain to their dying process. There is a time to let go. There is a time to decline heroic measures—and for Polly, this was that time.[54]

I called our children and their spouses to come to the hospital. Late that night we held hands around Polly's bed and asked God to hold her in his arms and gently take her home. Close to midnight I decided to go home, as Polly was sleeping quietly.

I got up early the next morning. As I was preparing my breakfast, I was listening to the same radio station as I had been a couple weeks previously. As I stood in my kitchen, looking out over our back yard, the spokesperson said, "You know, when it comes time to die, it's our relationships that will sustain us. The

relationships we cultivate today will sustain us then. We generally die the way we lived." How true. There is a sense in which
every day, every moment, we are preparing ourselves for the final
moments of our earthly life; and it's the relationships we have cultivated today with our loved ones, and most of all with the Lord,
that will strengthen and comfort us in life's final hours.

Earlier that morning I had read that day's selection from the
devotional "Our Daily Bread." The writer recounted the death
of his own daughter just a year prior to that date. He wrote: "We
needed the Christian community to guide us toward hope as we
stood at the funeral of a beloved young woman who had touched
so many lives with her smile, her godliness, her love of life, and
her care for others."[55]

I arrived at Polly's room about 8:00am. To my surprise, she
was awake and alert. I had not expected to find her so. Her eyes
followed me closely as I moved about in her room, arranging
things near her bed and setting her radio so she could listen to
some music.

At 8:43am her nurse entered the room and proceeded to prepare the morning's liquid "meal" through her feeding tube. I stood
on the opposite side of her bed. At 8:45am on August 6, 2003,

Polly quietly left her earthly "tent" and entered into the presence of her Lord and Savior, and of all her loved ones who had gone before. The long and unexpected journey she had been on for so many years had finally reached its earthly end.

Not everyone's passing is couched in quite the same set of circumstances as was Polly's. As a chaplain, I have seen more than my share of deaths that were anything but expected. Yet no one's passing is unexpected to God. Job said, *"Since his days are determined, the number of his months is with You; and his limits You have set so that he cannot pass"* (Job 14:5). The psalmist wrote: *Your eyes have seen my unformed substance; and in Your book were all written the days that were ordained for me, when as yet there was not one of them* (Psalm 139:16).

Psalm 116:15 tells us that *Precious in the sight of the Lord is the death of His godly ones.* The Lutheran commentator H. C. Leupold says that one of the things this means is that God "is manifestly watching over what takes place even when His saints are not rescued but seemingly perish."[56] This had certainly been true for us.

I do not pretend to understand the mysteries of God's providence, but I do know that in our case God knew and He prepared us for Polly's final days. At the end of such a long journey, the radio spokesperson's words on July 24, and the devotional in "Our Daily Bread" had been used by God to prepare me for what was about to transpire. July 25 *was* the last full day that Polly would spend in the nursing home—to linger for two weeks in the hospital, before entering into her eternal home in heaven. Now, she knew just how much better a place it truly is—better not only than the *painful* things of this life, but better than even the *best* things of this life, by far.

For I consider that the sufferings of this present time are not worthy to be compared with the glory that is to be revealed in us (Rom. 8:18).

Things which eye has not seen and ear has not heard, and which have not entered the heart of man, all that God has prepared for those who love Him (I Cor. 2:9).

Gone From My Sight

I'm standing on the seashore. A ship at my side

spreads her white sails to the morning breeze and starts

for the blue ocean.

She's an object of beauty and strength and I stand and

watch her

until, at length, she hangs like a speck of white cloud

just where the sea and the sky come down to mingle with

each other.

And then I hear someone at my side saying, "There, she's gone."

Gone where? Gone from my sight, that is all.

She is just as large in mast and hull and spar as she was

When she left my side.

And just as able to bear her load of living freight to the

place of destination.

Her diminished size is in *me*, not in her.

And just at the moment when someone at my side says,

"There, she is gone" there are other eyes watching her coming,

And there are other voices ready to take up the glad shout,

"Here she comes!"[57]

Henry Van Dyke

Rick and Polly – 1976

1973

Rick's mother and father visiting
Polly at her nursing home – 1994

1996

1996

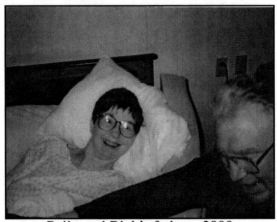

Polly and Rick's father - 2000

Part 3

AFTERMATH:
SOME PERSPECTIVES
ON GOD'S GRACE

Chapter XV

REFLECTIONS–GOD'S TRANSFORMING GRACE

A nyone who has lost a loved one knows that their passing is not the end of the story. For weeks and months, indeed for years, there is a process of reflecting on all that had transpired in the years before and consolidating the many lessons learned.

One of the things that family members do is remember their loved one's life, and their legacy. In Polly's case, she left to us the memory of a sweet, humble woman, who endured more than any of her friends could ever know, with a quiet faith in God that spoke more clearly than a thousand sermons.

Two days after Polly died, I passed a notebook to some of the nursing home staff who had assisted Polly the previous years.

Following are comments the staff logged in this notebook. Some of the comments included references to myself as Polly's husband and caregiver. I debated whether to include these. I decided not to delete all of them, as they reflect something of the love that I did have for Polly. She was not difficult to love.

"Polly lived at Brentwood III for a short time (four years) before she moved to another facility. Polly was a very cheerful person. Whenever you would see her she had a smile on her face that could cheer up the world. She was always complimenting others for things they do. She loved a challenge. She played a major part to our volleyball team. Although her health condition limited her to do some things by herself, she did as much as she could for herself, trying so hard to be independent as much as she could. I remember her face when she used to tell me that she was going out on pass to go to a ball game, she was so excited. She seemed to love baseball because she always kept up with the Rangers. Polly was a very kind and sweet individual who loved her family and she will be missed." Social worker

"I am so blessed to have known Polly. I only took care of her for a short time, but it was a special time. Every morning I would go into her room and say 'good morning Sunshine.' And she would smile so big.... If I did something like drop a cup of water she would laugh.... It has truly been a privilege to have met and cared for Polly. Rick...I am truly moved by the care and compassion for the way you took care of Polly. I am sorry for your loss, but am comforted knowing that she is with God in heaven and no longer suffering. God bless and take care." Nurse

"Polly was and still will be remembered as a special individual. She was fun and so full of life. Even if she could not move she made herself known that she was still there. It has been a privilege knowing both Polly and Rick. Thank you for enlightening my life with just knowing the two of you." Night nurse

"I may be wrong...but Polly was my pet. I always wanted her to be very well taken care of and comfortable. I want the best for all my residents, but it was different with Polly. She was one of my favorites.... It was a joy caring for Polly and a joy to see how Rick cared for Polly. My prayers are with the family at this time. We must find comfort in knowing that Polly is now at rest, and there is no more pain or suffering for her.... Again, I must say it was a joy to have cared for Polly and an inspiration all at the same time. It was a pleasure to have met you Rick, and I commend you! Stay strong. God is good...all the time. Keep your hand in his! Bless you and the rest of the family." Unit nurse

"Thank you for the privilege of knowing Polly. Her sense of humor and endurance motivated all the staff in our determination to continue in our chosen profession. Thank you Rick, for restoring my confidence in the institution of marriage and the spirit of love.... I shall miss both of you.... We've lost a member of our family, and pray your hearts will be comforted by the Spirit of God, as only He can console. Thank you for simply being who you and Polly are." Director of nursing

"Polly was an inspiration to me. She always had a smile as big as Texas. I will miss her sweet smile. God bless you Rick. Both of you will be missed. Polly loved life and will be missed by all." Medical aid

"Polly has been an inspiration to me. She had such a sweet disposition and spirit. I really wish I had known her before she lost her speech. She had her good days and bad days like everyone, and I always felt bad when I knew it was a bad day. She almost always gave me a smile and even laughed at my jokes. I loved it when she laughed out loud and got so tickled. Then we couldn't quit laughing. She will always be remembered. She made the world and this job better by knowing her. I will miss seeing that she watches her baseball games and turning off her radio. She will not be forgotten." Unit nurse

"It has been a privilege to have known Polly for the short time she was on my hall. She was not able to speak verbally, but she had a way of expressing herself with a smile or an occasional frown or a look of questioning.... Both of you will be missed. My prayers are with you." Unit nurse

"My heart goes out to Rick and the rest of the family. It is hard to lose a parent, but harder still to have to watch day by day the discomfort that they are in. God has his plans for people, and I believe that his plan for Polly was to infect everyone around her with her big beautiful smile. In the three years of helping take care of Polly I don't think there were times when she wouldn't have a big smile. She will be missed very much here." Unit nurse

"I feel privileged to have known Polly and Rick. Polly was never able to carry on a verbal conversation with me during the three years I knew her. But her non-verbal communication and laughter were quite clear. I know that Polly never seemed happier than when Rick walked into the room! Her face immediately lit up.... Polly had a wonderful sense of humor and I loved hearing her laugh at my silly jokes or when I would say something funny to her roommate. I am happy for Polly now because she is no longer imprisoned in her own body. She is free now. Praise God!... Thank you Rick for your devotion and care for Polly. And thank you Polly for your ongoing strength and courage and humor in the face of tragedy.... You both have changed my view, my perspective on life." Social worker

"The road in life is full of hills and valleys, highways winding and steep. But you and Polly climbed them together. Now Polly took the road to God's door. Now without pain or suffering. That door is beautiful. May God bless and keep you. I know this road was a tough one. God has a beautiful crown waiting for both of you full of his precious jewels. May God bless and keep you." Unit nurse

It would be very tempting to simply relay these comments, and allow you to believe that they reflected our innate worthiness of praise, but this would be quite misleading. By the time we arrived in the nursing home, the Lord had been working in our lives and hearts for many years. I well remember the years in the near wake of her diagnosis. These were years of struggling with discouragement and doubt. Our life seemed like one long, dark tunnel, with no relief in sight this side of heaven. From the merely human viewpoint, this is exactly what it was.

Some people, looking at our lives, probably saw it as being tragic in many ways; and certainly there was a very real tragic element. When I arrived at the end of Polly's life however, and looked back over the previous twenty years, I could only conclude that our life had indeed been a miracle of God's grace. No, there was no "big" miracle, in that Polly was never healed of her illness in this life, but there were many "little" miracles, in terms of God's sustaining us, guiding us, providing for us, strengthening and encouraging us, over the entire course of her illness—one day at a time. The promises of Psalm 55:22 and 68:19 had proven true. God had indeed sustained us. He had carried us, and our burden, each day of our life, to the very last day of Polly's life on earth—and that is no "small" miracle in my estimation. The psalmist said, *We have thought on Your lovingkindness, O God....As is Your name, O God, So is Your praise to the ends of the earth; Your right hand is full of righteousness.... For such is God, Our God forever and ever; He will guide us until death* (Psalm 48:9-10, 14).

Even more than that, God was at work all through these years, renewing and reshaping our hearts. At least I knew this was the case in my own life. A couple weeks after Polly's passing, my daughter and I were out for lunch together. We were walking through our local mall, and talking. She is a remarkably sweet young lady. She said to me, "Dad, I think the reason God put you with Mom was because He knew you had the qualities necessary to care for her." Well, I knew myself better than she did. I replied, "You know, I think one reason God put me with your mom, was because He knew I needed to *acquire* the qualities necessary to care for her." It's true. Not that I have "arrived" or never struggle with my own selfish tendencies. I do—and this side of heaven I always will. I realized, however, that God had been at work using these serious difficulties to further his work in my heart. It's not the difficulties themselves that reshape us. Apart from the Lord, affliction can destroy us. Yet with God, they can be as instruments in the hands of a wise surgeon—a surgeon of the heart.

It's been observed that the fruit of the Spirit described in Galatians 5 is cultivated in large measure in the midst of affliction, and I believe it's true.[58] It's not difficult to love those who love us, but it takes the Spirit of God to love when love is not returned. It's easy to experience joy when things are enjoyable, but it takes the Spirit of God to find reason for joy when things are less than pleasant in our life. Anyone can be at peace when things are peaceful, but it takes the Spirit of God to instill peace in our hearts in the midst of life's storms. It's not hard to be patient when our needs and desires are met, but it takes the Spirit of God to help us be patient when we must wait, and wait, and wait. It's easy to be kind to those who are kind to us, but it takes the Spirit of God to return kindness to those who are wanting in this grace. It's easy to be devoted to what is good when everyone else shares our values, but it takes the Spirit of God to remain devoted to what is good when our culture is promoting evil. When life is easy it's not hard to be faithful, but it takes the Spirit of God to remain faithful when we could avoid much trouble by going back on our word. It's not hard to be gentle with those who are gentle with us, but when we're tempted to lash out in anger, it takes the Spirit of God to give us a gentle (though firm) response. It takes the Spirit of God to grant us self-control, when it would be much easier to give in to our sinful impulses. The flip side of this matter is that affliction may also be used by God, not only to instill in our hearts godly virtues, but also to prevent us from falling into sin. This was true for the Apostle Paul, whose "thorn in the flesh" was used by God to keep him from sinful pride (II Cor. 12:7).

I will be honest in saying that in the early days it was not always easy to demonstrate patience in ways I wish I had. Affliction has a way of forcing us to deal with our hearts. I learned that only by opening our hearts to the Lord on a daily basis can we experience the changes only He can bring. I learned that far more important to God than our personal comfort is our personal holiness—and He knows how to use affliction to instill in us qualities we would otherwise never possess.

It was on a spring day in 1990 I believe, that it seemed that the Lord spoke directly to me about how much Polly was really suffering. I knew this. Yet I also at times was naturally more focused on how her illness was affecting my own life—and it was. My life had been completely turned upside down by what had happened to Polly. On that day, however, I realized in a new way that how her illness was affecting *my* life was next to nothing compared to how it was affecting *her* life. I distinctly recall saying in my heart, "Lord, please help me never again to say an impatient word to Polly." By God's grace, I can honestly say I don't believe I ever did.

I loved Polly when I married her, but when I laid her body to rest nearly 32 years later, I had learned to love her in a completely different way. Scripture tells us that there are three virtues which

God is instilling in his children above all others: *faith, hope, and love*. We are told, however, that *the greatest of these is love* (I Cor. 13:13)—a love that seeks the highest good of the other, even at great cost to oneself if that is what's required. Such love comes only from the Lord.

In reflecting on the years of Polly's illness, it occurred to me that God was at work in at least three ways during those years. First, there were many things that He was doing *for* us. He had been preparing us, guiding us, providing for us at so many turns in our life. In spite of the unexplained suffering, God had truly been with us. Secondly, God had been at work *in* us. It was obvious that He was at work in Polly's life; and I knew this was true for me as well. He had been at work in our hearts, changing us and shaping us.

Lastly, we would come to see that God was also working *through* us, in ways far beyond our ability to comprehend. I realized that He was using our affliction to demonstrate to others something of his own mercy and faithfulness in our lives. This is no doubt true on the human level, but it is true also on the spiritual level. The Bible tells us that our lives are bearing witness to the trustworthiness of God even to those beings who inhabit the spiritual realm. This was certainly true for Job (cf. Job 1-2). His life demonstrated that Satan's accusations were unfounded. It is true for us as well. Paul says that God's wisdom is *being made known through the church to the rulers and the authorities in the heavenly places* (Eph. 3:10). Even if no one else sees what God is doing in our life, the angelic and demonic hosts do. One day we will know just how much this may be true.[59]

Some years before Polly's passing, I was reading through John's Gospel. I came to John 21:19, in which are recorded the words of Jesus regarding *by what kind of death* Peter would *glorify God*. The wording of this verse struck me, because though I had often thought of how our *life* could bring glory to God, I had never really thought about how our *death* (or our loved one's death) could glorify God. From that day on, I prayed almost daily that when it came time for Polly to depart from us, God would be glorified in some way. I believe He answered that prayer. I believe that God was glorified not only in Polly's life, but also in her death.

Sometimes, when I think over Polly's life, I'm overwhelmed by the memories. I have recorded only some of the difficulties she faced, and that we faced together. Yet when I think of all that God did *for* us as well as *in* us, I'm overwhelmed by the memories of his mercy and grace.

Soli Deo Gloria.

Chapter XVI

WHEN LIFE SEEMS UNFAIR—
GOD'S SUSTAINING GRACE

I t may seem that this might be the place where I should conclude this book, but there are some things that I believe should
not be left out. One is the matter of our faith in God in the face of
suffering. There is no way that anyone can navigate the kind of
journey that Polly did without their faith in God being tested—and
I must say that our faith was indeed tested, at times severely. As a
hospital chaplain I have sat with countless patients who have asked
me, "What did I do to deserve this?" I have not found answers to
come easy. One of the things I appreciate so much about God's
word is that it is honest. It does not dodge the hard questions in
life, including the question of suffering.

One of the passages that encouraged me the most during the course of our experience was Psalm 73. In this psalm, Asaph records for us his own crisis of faith in light of suffering. Asaph's words have helped me. I hope they will be helpful to you as well.

This psalm opens the third book of the Psalms. It is identified as *A Psalm of Asaph.* This would imply that it was written by the musician and worship leader who served during David's reign (I Chron. 15:16, 25). He begins with a confession. First a confession of faith: *Surely God is good to Israel, To those who are pure in heart!* This is something every God-fearing Israelite believed— that God would bless his covenant people and extend his goodness to them. However, he then voices a confession of doubt: *But as for me, my feet came close to stumbling, My steps had almost slipped.* He had come near to straying away from the path of loyalty to God, and of being numbered among the *pure in heart.* He tells us why: *For I was envious of the arrogant As I saw the prosperity of the wicked.* Asaph had noticed that those who had abandoned God were nonetheless doing quite well. It seemed as though God was being good to them; and he was envious.

Asaph then describes the *arrogant* and *wicked* in some detail. First he describes the circumstances of their life. *For there are no pains in their death, And their body is fat.* Their health is not in jeopardy; nor do they lack for anything their appetite desires. *They are not in trouble as other men, Nor are they plagued like mankind.* They are not threatened by disabling or painful afflictions, as are many others.

Then he describes the attitude of their heart. *Therefore pride is their necklace; The garment of violence covers them.* Assuming that they are the cause of their own success, they exhibit a proud demeanor; and they see others as people to be used or abused, simply tools to be used for promoting their own happiness. *Their eye bulges from fatness; The imaginations of their heart run riot.* They are "living large" and their look betrays a corrupt heart.

Asaph particularly pays attention to their speech. *They mock and wickedly speak of oppression; They speak from on high.* They openly declare their plans to oppress others. They speak as though there is no one higher than themselves. *They have set their mouth against the heavens, And their tongue parades through the earth.* Not only do they threaten others, but they speak against God as well. Their evil speech is unrestrained.

Therefore his people return to this place, And waters of abundance are drunk by them. This verse is a bit enigmatic, but perhaps

Asaph is noting that these folk attract quite a following—a following of people who appear to be enjoying the "good life" as a result of following in their steps.

They say, "How does God know? And is there knowledge with the Most High?" When they are confronted with the idea that God takes note of their evil lives, and will intervene to judge them, they mock the very idea.

Behold, these are the wicked; And always at ease, they have increased in wealth. Asaph has well described the carefree lives of the ungodly, driving home the reason for his envy.

In stark contrast, he describes his own life: *Surely in vain I have kept my heart pure And washed my hands in innocence; For I have been stricken all day long And chastened every morning.* Though he does not tell us what the affliction is that he is referring to, it is obviously severe and relentless. Not a day or hour goes by that he is not under the weight of whatever this burden might be. Consequently, he feels that his efforts to live a life cleansed from sin have been *in vain.* It's been for nothing.

Though Asaph entertained these thoughts in his heart, he had restrained himself from openly declaring them. *If I had said, "I will speak thus," Behold, I would have betrayed the generation of*

Your children. He wanted to maintain at least an outward example of faith, if for no other reason than to keep from contributing to the spiritual ruin of others. Nonetheless, he says: *When I pondered to understand this, It was troublesome in my sight.*

Asaph has given voice to thoughts that millions of others have entertained. Why is it that so often those who do evil prosper, and the innocent suffer severe affliction? It seems that the scales of justice have been reversed. I remember being asked by a brother in Africa one time, what's the point of following Christ if as a result we are not spared from suffering. The very question betrays a common misunderstanding. Have you ever thought what the world would be like if those who sinned were immediately judged, and those who sought to follow God were spared from suffering? What would this say about our motivation in obeying the Lord? As has been said, in such a world "only fools and masochists would sin."[60] On the contrary, those who followed the Lord would be suspected of doing so primarily for their own immediate benefit. Yet isn't this exactly what Satan accused Job of when he asked, *Does Job fear God for nothing?* (Job 1:9). In other words, he accused Job of fearing God merely for his own benefit, to escape affliction and secure his temporal blessings. He was certain that if God removed his blessings from Job, he would curse Him. It's not difficult to trust and fear God when all is going well, but when God allows us to suffer, our faith is tested. When this happens, the motivation of our heart is more fully revealed and refined. In one way or another, the faith of all God's people will be tested and sifted in this life; and this is what was happening to Asaph. He was troubled in heart—until he came *into the sanctuary of God.*

The psalm, and the survival of Asaph's faith, hinges on this little word *until.* It was when Asaph drew near to God in the place of worship and fellowship with Him, that he began to find peace of mind and heart. Perhaps it was during a season of worship that Asaph found his perspective on life changing. Or it may simply have been during a time of meditation and reflection on God, or as the result of conversation with one of the priests, that his thinking was reframed. The same can be true for us. When we face trouble in life—major trouble—we have a choice, either to pull away from God or to move toward Him. Asaph chose the latter way—and so must we, if we are to hope ever to find an answer to the seeming inequities of our lives.

It was in *the sanctuary* that God guided Asaph toward a different perspective on his situation in life. The first thing He showed him was something about the ungodly. He writes, *Then I perceived their end.* God reminded him of the ultimate outcome of their way of life. He describes it in vivid terms. *Surely You set them in slippery places; You cast them down to destruction. How they are destroyed in a moment! They are utterly swept away by sudden terrors! Like a dream when one awakes, O Lord, when aroused, You will despise their form.* He describes the Lord's judgment on the godless as one of complete and sudden destruction. One day they would "awake" from their life as if it was only a "dream," to experience the reality of God's judgment. God is a long-suffering God, who offers his grace to all, but those who become hardened in rejecting his grace will ultimately experience his justice.

When my heart was embittered And I was pierced within, Then I was senseless and ignorant; I was like a beast before You. Asaph confesses that when he allowed his heart to become bitter, and he was envious of the ungodly, he was little more than an ignorant beast in his attitude toward God. Wild animals apparently have little if any perception of the ultimate outcome of their lives. They're just concerned with what appears before them now — and so sometimes are we.

Now however, in addition to the Lord's reminding Asaph something about the ungodly, He reminds him of something about himself, about his own life. *Nevertheless I am continually with You.* Despite the fact that his situation had not yet changed, this was something that would always be true. The Lord was with him. He had not been abandoned. He was continually in God's **presence**. When Jacob was fleeing for his life from his brother Esau, the Lord gave him a vision of himself in a dream. In it He said to Jacob, *Behold, I am with you and will keep you wherever you go, and will bring you back to this land; for I will not leave you until I have done what I have promised you* (Gen. 28:15). Has not the Lord assured us of his presence, and promised never to leave us or forsake us, no matter what life may bring (Rom. 8:35-39)?

Not only was God with Asaph, but he was in his **grasp**. *You have taken hold of my right hand.* Such a statement implies not only God's presence, but his help in our weakness. Those of us who have been parents recall how when our children were little, and we were about to cross a busy street with them at our side, we didn't wait for them to grab our hand. We took hold of their hand, and we did not let go, until we were well across the street. So it is with the Lord. Jesus said that no one will ever be able to snatch us out of his hand, or the Father's hand, for He is *greater than all* (John 10:29).

Not only was Asaph in God's presence and in his grasp, but he was also under God's **guidance**. *With Your counsel You will guide me*. It's possible to see this statement as speaking of God's provision of counsel or wisdom in the midst of life's struggles; and this would not be wrong. James tells us to ask God for wisdom when we are facing life's trials (James 1: 5). However, it is perhaps best to see this statement as promising that God will guide us through to the fulfillment of his good purposes for our life. One commentator renders this phrase: *In your purpose you will lead me*.[61] No matter how things may look for the moment, God will fulfill his plans and purposes for us. What a wonderful assurance.

And afterward (You will) *receive me to glory.* This is the last thing Asaph was reminded of, that God's ultimate purpose would be to bring him to a place of honor and **glory**. Though some see this as a promise of God's ultimately bringing Asaph to a place of honor in this life, it seems difficult to escape the fact that for many this will not be fulfilled til their days on earth are ended. In contrast to the ultimate destiny of the ungodly (*destruction*), Asaph was headed for *glory*. So is it true for all of us who know the Lord.

If we belong to Him, we are constantly in God's presence, in his grasp, assured of the fulfillment of his purpose for us, and destined to enter into his glory.

Asaph then proceeds to describe that glorious destination. *Whom have I in heaven but You? And besides You, I desire nothing on earth.* Though at present he may lack certain earthly blessings, these are nothing compared to having God at his side. Certainly, we enjoy the earthly blessings of God we are granted. Yet even the best of these blessings fade into nothingness when compared to knowing the Giver of every good gift. This can be one of the functions of affliction in our life, to magnify our love for God above our love of his good gifts.

My flesh and my heart may fail, But God is the strength of my heart and my portion forever. Though Asaph's outer as well as inner resources may be exhausted, God's supply will never come to an end.

Asaph now summarizes his findings. *For, behold, those who are far from You will perish. You have destroyed all those who are unfaithful to You.* Though he had previously envied such people, he now saw that they are more to be pitied. *But as for me, the nearness of God is my good.* This is the most significant statement of this psalm. Do you recall how Asaph opened this psalm, with his confession that *God is good to Israel, To those who are pure in heart?* Well, in this statement he reveals what he had learned about God's goodness. He had learned that the greatest good God can give to anyone isn't a prosperous life, or a trouble-free life. No, the greatest good God can give anyone is Himself. He is the God who is mysteriously working out his purposes, even in the midst of life's tragic inequities. He is the God who will ultimately set everything right. He is the God whose presence is worth far more than every earthly blessing. It is because of these truths that Asaph is able to close his psalm with these words: *I have made the Lord God my refuge, That I may tell of all Your works.* Rather than turning away, he has drawn near to God to find solace in Him. As a result he found reason to tell others of God's many works of grace. Perhaps not the "big" miracle of complete and immediate deliverance from all his troubles, but a thousand "little" miracles of God's carrying him through life's storms to the safe haven of his glory.

Scripture tells us that in ways beyond our comprehension God is able to use the evil and suffering we experience in this world in the accomplishment of his good purposes. This is stated very clearly in Paul's words recorded in Romans 8:28, *And we know that God causes all things to work together for good to those who love God, to those who are called according to His purpose.* This does not mean that all things *are* good, but it does say that God uses all things *for* the ultimate good of his children. Some of them are things which God in fact hates, and will one day bring into judgment. Yet they are not beyond the scope of his gracious purposes. As Joni Eareckson Tada has written: "God permits what he hates to achieve what he loves."[62]

In grappling with this issue, Old Testament scholar John Goldingay writes: "At first sight the belief that God is behind the trouble that comes to us is a frightening doctrine: what kind of a God is this, whose purpose includes so much distress? But the alternative—a God whose purpose is continually being frustrated by evil—is even more frightening. Better a God whose mystery we cannot understand (but who has given us grounds for trusting when we cannot understand) than one whose adequacy we cannot rely on, or whose interest we cannot be sure of."[63]

This truth was illustrated in the case of Joseph, who was brutally betrayed by his jealous brothers, sold into slavery and eventually confined to prison on a slanderous charge. At the end of his life however, when he encountered his brothers, he was able to say,

As for you, you meant evil against me, but God meant it for good in order to bring about this present result, to preserve many people alive (Genesis 50:20). During all the years of trial and struggle, he had no glimpse of what good God could possibly bring out of his affliction. It wasn't until later in life that he could look back and see what God had done. While he was waiting for his faith to become sight, he undoubtedly trusted in the unchanging character of the God he had learned to trust as a young boy.

The truth of God's providence was also, and in supreme fashion, demonstrated in the cross of Christ. In his Pentecostal sermon, Peter declared concerning Jesus that *this Man, delivered over by the predetermined plan and foreknowledge of God, you nailed to a cross by the hands of godless men and put Him to death* (Acts 2:23). The most heinous crime committed in human history, God used to accomplish his greatest good—the redemption of all who would place their faith in Christ.

During this life we do not know all of God's purposes in our sufferings. It has been pointed out that if Job had been aware of all the reasons for his trials, it would not have been nearly the test of faith that it was.[64] It would certainly have been a test of patience, but not a test of faith.

I do believe, however, that there are some of God's purposes which we can comprehend, and which can only be accomplished in the midst of such a world as ours. What if there are some things about God Himself that we could never know or experience, or appreciate apart from living in a world like this? In what other kind of world could we experience God's compassion and mercy on suffering, or his grace and love toward sinners like ourselves, or his ability to deliver when all hope is lost, or to sustain when all strength is gone, to comfort when we have suffered great loss, to provide when all resources are exhausted, or experience his holiness and justice in ultimately defeating evil, as well as his wisdom in using it for his glory and the ultimate good of those who love Him? In what other kind of world could we know such things about God?

What if by allowing us to live in such our world, that God is also instilling in us some qualities that could be formed in no other kind of world than one like this? Qualities like humility, dependence and faith when we do not fully understand, compassion on others who are suffering affliction, grace toward those who have sinned against us, generosity and even sacrifice for the benefit of those who are suffering great want, perseverance when things are so hard we feel like giving up, hatred of sin and its horrific consequences, gratitude for God's blessings after a season of deprivation or even despair, a hunger in our heart for a better world to come—and when it finally does arrive, joy inexpressible as a result of our participation in God's triumph over his foes. These are the kinds of qualities that we remember people for after they are gone, and which we speak of at their funerals. Yet they would not even exist in a world that was much different than the one in which we live.

Don't think for a moment that God is untouched by the pain of our suffering. The prophet Isaiah said of Israel, *In all their affliction He was afflicted* (Isaiah 63:9). It was, however, supremely in the incarnation of his Son Jesus that God experienced the fullest measure of human pain and suffering. As a man, he likely endured the loss of his earthly father Joseph during his youth, and later rejection by members of his family. He endured opposition from the religious leaders of his nation, as well as abandonment by his disciples, and betrayal by one of his closest companions. He was falsely accused, unjustly tried and condemned, severely beaten, publicly humiliated, and shamelessly executed in the most agonizing manner humanly conceived. As Dorothy Sayers once said, speaking of our gracious God: "He can exact nothing from us that he has not exacted from himself. He has himself gone through the whole human experience, from the trivial irritations of family life and the cramping restrictions of hard work and lack of money to the worst horrors of pain and humiliation, defeat, despair, and death."[65]

This does not mean we should just passively acquiesce in the face of suffering, and consider it "all good." Not in the least. The words of Christian ethicist Dr. John Kilner were helpful to me: "With so much to gain, it might seem worthwhile to promote suffering in one's life. However, just as people find life only by losing it, so people gain the value of suffering only when they oppose suffering as a genuine evil (albeit helplessly) and yet experience the goodness of God in its midst."[66] The words of Dr. Paul Tournier were similarly helpful. "The person matures, develops...not because of the deprivation (affliction) itself, but through his own active response to misfortune, through the struggle to come to terms with it and morally to overcome it—even if in spite of everything there is no cure."[67] Though evil and suffering are not good in themselves, God can use them to accomplish what is good in our lives.

None of this is meant to deny or minimize the pain that people feel now. Nor is it to say that we should not do what we can to avoid unnecessary suffering (insofar as it is consistent with being faithful to God). When David was threatened by King Saul, he said to himself: *Now I will perish one day by the hand of Saul. There is nothing better for me than to escape into the land* of *the Philistines* (I Sam. 27:1). When Mary and Joseph were threatened by Herod's violent anger, they fled to Egypt, under divine direction (Mt. 2:13). When Jesus heard about the execution of John the Baptist, *he withdrew...to a secluded place by Himself* (Mt. 14:13). When the Jewish leaders threatened to stone Jesus, He *hid himself and went out of the temple* (Jn. 8:59b). When He heard that they were plotting his death, *Jesus no longer continued to walk publicly among the Jews, but went away from there to the country near the wilderness, into a city called Ephraim; and there He stayed with the disciples* (Jn. 11:54). It's proper to flee from unnecessary suffering.[68]

Nor does this mean that we should not do what we can to alleviate suffering (our own and others). We should. However, it is to say that the suffering that we cannot avoid or alleviate is not without meaning—nor beyond its ultimate relief. As I wrote in the Introduction: Affliction is the crucible in which our faith is tested, but it is also the crucible in which God's faithfulness is proven. This was a truth that over the course of our life God was seeking to help us comprehend, not just in our mind, but in our life and heart as well.[69]

Chapter XVII

LETTING GO AND MOVING ON— GOD'S COMFORTING GRACE

T hough as a hospital chaplain I had done an immense amount of reading about "grief and loss," and though I had witnessed the grief of countless people in the hospital over the years, I was quite unprepared for the experience of grieving the loss of Polly. I had been told on occasion that it's not normal for believing Christians to grieve—that somehow God's grace preserves us from the pain of loss.[70] I have found however, both from observation and now from experience, that this is not really so. Neither is it biblical for us to expect that it should be.

J. I. Packer wrote: "The idea, sometimes voiced, that because Christians know death to be for believers the gate of glory, they will therefore not grieve at times of bereavement is inhuman non-sense.... Grief is the human system reacting to the pain of loss, and as such it is an inescapable reaction."[71]

The first person described as grieving in the Bible is God Himself. We are told in Genesis that when the Lord observed the extent of the evil in the ante-deluvian world, *He was grieved in His heart* (6:6). In fact, the Holy Spirit and God the Son are also described in Scripture as grieving. Isaiah, in describing Israel, said: *But they rebelled and grieved His Holy Spirit* (Isa. 63:10a). Jesus was *a man of sorrows, and acquainted with grief* (Isa. 53:3), which was evidenced in his life on more than one occasion. *When He approached Jerusalem, He saw the city and wept over it* (Luke 19:41). When He approached the burial place of his friend Lazarus, we are told that *He was deeply moved in spirit and was troubled*, and that He *wept* (John 11:33, 35). Certainly, the description of the emotions of the Godhead are not intended to teach us that God is like us in this regard. These statements are not, however, without meaning. At the least, they imply that God identifies with our sorrow.

Not only is God described as grieving, but God's people are described as grieving as well. When Sarah died, we are told that

Abraham *went in to mourn for Sarah and to weep for her* (Gen. 23:2b). When Jacob died, we are told that Joseph *fell on his father's face, and wept over him and kissed him* (Gen. 50:1). When Moses died, it is written that the nation Israel *wept for Moses in the plains of Moab thirty days* (Deut. 34:8). When Stephen perished at the hands of his countrymen, we are told that *Some devout men buried Stephen, and made loud lamentation over him* (Acts 8:2).

One day, God will wipe away all our tears (Isa. 25:8; Rev. 21:4), but that time is not yet. Until then, though we do not grieve in the same way as those who have no hope (I Thess. 4:13), nevertheless, we do grieve.

Israel was forbidden from expressing her grief in ways characteristic of the surrounding pagan nations. They were instructed not to cut themselves, or shave their heads when their loved ones died (Lev. 19:28; Deut. 14:1). However, they did have mourning practices of their own, which included covering their head (II Sam. 15:30), going barefoot (Isa. 20:2), and covering their lips (Lev. 13:45; Micah 3:7). The fact that Ezekiel was forbidden such expressions upon the death of his wife, as a sign of judgment on the nation Israel (Ezek. 24:16-17), shows that such restraint was not considered normal.

Perhaps we find a model for our grieving in the reaction of Job to the great tragedies he experienced. When he was first informed of the death of his children, the text reads: *Then Job arose and tore his robe and shaved his head, and he fell to the ground and worshiped* (Job 1:20). Grieving profoundly, but worshiping humbly.[72] Perhaps we will not be able to express ourselves in precisely this way all at once; but in time, we can expect God's Spirit to help us do so.

The first time I found myself alone after Polly's death, I sat down and wept. Thirty-two years of married life unfolded before my eyes. The years of adjustment and of bright hopes. The years of child raising. The years of disappointment and pain. The years of laughter and joy. The long years of her slow decline. They were all now a thing of the past; and she was gone. For the remainder of my days on this earth the one who knew me best, and whom I knew best, was to be no longer here. I have seen patients in the hospital who have lost a leg, by accident or surgery, and it is understandably very painful. Why should we think that the loss of one who had occupied part of our heart should be any less so? When the friends of Lazarus witnessed the tears of Jesus at his tomb, they said, *See how He loved him* (John 11:36). Tears of grief are most often tears of love.

The tears were more frequent and intense during those first few months. Though they became less so with the passage of time, still there were occasions when they returned, sometimes with great force. They returned when I visited places that held significant memories for us. The first time I visited her nursing home, I could stay no more than five minutes. The memories were too overwhelming. When I returned to a fast food establishment where I had brought Polly on Saturday mornings for several years, to buy and feed her breakfast, I could not stay long enough to order a meal. When special times came around, I found the tears returning as well. Her birthday. Our wedding anniversary. When the anniversary of her passing came, I found myself reliving the events—actually for many years thereafter. I learned in time to plan to take that day off from visiting in the hospital.

I realized, however, that I could not go on avoiding places that were charged with emotional memories. So I decided to return to her nursing home once a week, to see the staff who had been my family, and to visit with some of the other residents. In fact, for a year and a half I visited once a week an elderly lady who lived across the hall from Polly—until she also died. Her family asked me to conduct her graveside memorial, which I gladly did.

There's a curious verse in that most enigmatic of books, Ecclesiastes. It says, *Sorrow is better than laughter, for by a sad countenance the heart is made better* (Eccl. 7:3 NKJV). This might seem to be a contradiction. What the writer is apparently saying, however, is that a sorrowful heart is healed not by forced cheerfulness, but by giving expression to its grief. It has been said that "the cure for grief is grieving"—and it's largely true.[73] That's why the apostle Paul instructs us to *weep with those who weep* (Rom. 12:15b). Not everyone finds it natural to do so. Certainly, not every time or place is most appropriate for giving open expression to our grief, but it is biblical wisdom to find a place where we *can* give expression to our sorrow, and to ask God to give us a friend who will at the very least listen to our tears.

I found immense comfort in giving myself permission to weep, when the tears would naturally come. I also found comfort in simply telling our story to others. I did it mostly through writing. As time went by, however, I found that people wanted to hear our story; and I gradually found the courage to tell it on occasion to various groups.

The first couple years after Polly's passing, I felt like I was walking backward. I was almost entirely oriented to the past and where I had been in life. This is as it should be. It takes time to process the past, and for its lessons to be integrated into our life. The most pressing question I asked myself during these years was "Who am I?" That may seem strange, but for many years I had assumed the identity of my wife's caregiver. For a long time, when people asked me what I did, I told them what my work was at the time. Inside however, I was telling myself, "I take care of my wife. I'm my wife's caregiver. That's who I am." Now, however, that was no longer true. I knew who I wasn't anymore, but I really wasn't sure who I was.

For the next two years I felt like I was walking sideways. I was thinking to myself, "Okay. What now?" I was oriented to the present and thinking of what God wanted me to do each day. Then, after four years, I found myself walking forward into the future, and asking myself, "What's next?" I would never be the same person I was before we had begun this long journey. The experience had forever shaped my life. Yet now I was beginning to move into the future, and anticipating what God had still for me to do this side of heaven.

The reality of grief notwithstanding, the process of "letting go and moving on" need not be all "sorrow and tears." Jesus pronounced a blessing on those who mourn, that they would be comforted (Mt. 5:4). In fact, one of the purposes for which the Messiah came into the world was *to comfort all who mourn* (Isa. 61:2b). I now know that there is indeed a comforting grace that comes from God alone—but it's a grace that comes through various means.

Some of God's comfort comes through the friends He gives us. Paul recounts how when he was depressed about recent experiences in his life and ministry, God encouraged him through his friend Titus. *But God, who comforts the depressed, comforted us through the coming of Titus* (II Cor. 7:6). The Lord gave me a few friends who were simply willing to listen as I told our story and shared how I was feeling. Many times over the years, after simply sitting and listening to a grieving patient in the hospital, they had said to me, "Thank you so much just for listening." Now I knew just how encouraging such a friend could be.

Some of God's comfort comes through the promises of his Word. The psalmist says, *This is my comfort in my affliction, that your word has revived me* (Ps. 119:50). Paul tells us that *through perseverance and the encouragement of the Scriptures we...have hope* (Rom. 15:4). God had brought such encouragement through the Psalms when Polly was first diagnosed; and now I found that He did the same when she departed. In reading through the book of Genesis, I came across two passages that brought real comfort to me. Just before Jacob died, he spoke to his son Joseph and said, *Behold, I am about to die,* **but God will be with you,** *and bring you back to the land of your fathers* (Gen. 48:21). Years later, when Joseph was also about to die, he said similar words to his brothers: *I am about to die,* **but God will surely take care of you** *and bring you up from this land to the land which He promised on oath to Abraham, to Isaac and to Jacob* (Gen. 50:24). I found that though my dear wife was no longer with me, God was. Even though I did not know where I was going, He did.[74]

There is an instructive story in the Old Testament that encouraged me during these years. It's the story of David and his men suffering the loss of almost all they possessed in this world. It's recorded in I Samuel 30:1-6. *Then it happened when David and his men came to Ziklag on the third day, that the Amalekites had made a raid on the Negev and on Ziklag, and had overthrown Ziklag and burned it with fire; and they took captive the women and all who were in it, both small and great, without killing anyone, and carried them off and went their way. When David and his men came to the city, behold, it was burned with fire, and their wives and their sons and their daughters had been taken captive. Then David and the people who were with him lifted their voices and wept until there was no strength in them to weep. Now David's two wives had been taken captive, Ahinoam the Jezreelitess and Abigail the widow of Nabal the Carmelite. Moreover David was greatly distressed because the people spoke of stoning him, for all the people were embittered, each one because of his sons and his daughters. But David strengthened himself in the Lord his God.*

It's obvious why these men wept—and *wept until there was no strength in them to weep.* We would think there was something wrong with them if they had not. What's instructive, however, in this passage is the last line: *But David strengthened himself in the Lord his God.* He found strength to take action to respond to this crisis, not in himself, but in the Lord. I remember a friend who had previously lost his wife to cancer, telling me not too long before Polly died, "Rick, when Polly passes, your recovery will be your own responsibility."[75] I never forgot that. Though God can use others to help us in our recovery through grief, this is something we cannot expect others to accomplish for us. It is something we must take responsibility for ourselves. We must find in our relationship with the Lord, however, the strength it will require.

Some of you who read this have endured losses of a more traumatic nature than most. You lost a child, or a loved one in a tragic accident, or worse. It was anything but expected; and it has left you with a wound that seems like it will never heal. We are not promised that all our tears will be dried in this lifetime. Total healing awaits God's final intervention in history (Isa. 25:8; Rev. 21:4). Yet God is not unaware of your sorrow; and in time He can ease your pain. What's more, this side of heaven, He can use the empathy and compassion that your grief has instilled in your heart to enable you to come along side others who are walking the path of grief.

The day before Polly's passing the following devotional by Dave Branon appeared in "Our Daily Bread." Once again, I found God speaking to me through its words in such a timely way.

"Since 1988, I've enjoyed writing several *Our Daily Bread* articles each month. I've felt blessed to dig into Scripture, observe life, and provide spiritual help in this publication.... But on June 6, 2002, I found myself unable to offer help. On the last day of her junior year of high school, our 17-year-old daughter Melissa was killed in a car accident.... In one horrible instant, everything we knew about God and the Bible and heaven was put to the test. We needed the Christian community to guide us toward hope as we stood at the funeral of a beloved young woman who had touched so many lives with her smile, her godliness, her love of life, and her care for others.... For many weeks, I couldn't write. What could I say? How could I find words to help others when my family—when I—needed so much?.... Now, months later as I begin to write again, I can say that God has not changed. He is still our loving heavenly Father, the 'God of all comfort' (2 Corinthians 1:3). He is still the source of hope in the face of unexpected grief. I write of Him with a renewed sense of my need for His touch, His love, His strength. Broken, I write of the only One who can make us whole"[76] He is indeed the "source of hope in the face of unexpected grief."

A year after Polly's death, I decided to take two weeks and visit people and places in the Pacific Northwest that had been meaningful to us in the early years of our marriage. I flew from Dallas to Seattle, arriving on a Saturday. The next morning, my hosts Dan and Carolyn Brannen, took me to their church, Mercer Island Covenant. I made myself comfortable in the back row of the auditorium. As the worship team opened the service, they began with a song that I had never heard in a Sunday worship service, and never have since — but it was the very song that we had chosen as the background to the video of pictures of Polly's life which we showed at her memorial service a year before. I thought to myself, "How appropriate." About twenty minutes later the pastor stood and opened his message with a story about a minister in the Covenant denomination of a previous generation. As the story unfolded, it became evident that the story was about my grandfather, Dr. Paul Rood. He had been the pastor of the First Covenant Church of Seattle in the 1920s. The pastor didn't know I was there. In fact, he didn't even know who I was, until I introduced myself to him after the service as Paul Rood's grandson.

A few years later I was home in Dallas and received an invitation to attend a dinner in honor of a local ministry to the people of China headed by a pastor who was a personal friend. I got a little lost looking for the restaurant where the dinner was held. When I arrived, I was directed to my assigned table. There was one seat left, to the right of a couple I had never met. I learned that they had served as missionaries to Vietnam and other parts of Asia. After introducing myself to this couple, they asked, "Are you married?"

I replied, "I used to be, but my wife passed away a few years ago." They asked me what had happened to her. When I told them she had Huntington's Disease, they seemed astonished. The husband said to me, "My mother died from Huntington's as well!"

As it turned out, the wife was an editor for a Christian periodical to the Chinese world. She later asked if I would write an article for their magazine, telling something of our story. Of course, I did. If I had been seated at any other table, or at any other seat, it's highly unlikely that I would ever have met this couple, or been given this opportunity to minister to others.

When I had left the worship service in Seattle a few years before, and now when I left this dinner where I met this couple, on both occasions it was as though the Lord was saying to me, "Rick, I'm with you; and you're exactly where I want you to be." It's all I really needed to know; and ten years later, I can tell you that it still is.

Chapter XVIII

THE HOPE OF GLORY—GOD'S FUTURE GRACE [77]

O ne of the things that accompany the absence of someone
you love is an increased interest in what it must be like for
them in heaven. I certainly found my mind gravitating to thoughts
of heaven in the days and months following Polly's passing. In
this final chapter I want to share some of the thoughts of heaven
that occurred to me during that first year.

I wondered first what it must have been like for Polly to
enter heaven—what the first minutes and hours must have been
like. Jesus spoke of angels escorting the souls of believers to
heaven (Luke 16:22). I've spoken to patients in the hospital who
claim to have seen their deceased loved ones during "near death

encounters."[78] I don't know for sure what to make of this—whether our loved ones really do come to help escort us to heaven—but I know of no reason to doubt it. If so, it certainly would ease the transition from this life to the next. Certainly, they must be among the first to greet us once we arrive. Can't you see the tears and hear the exclamations of joy and love? There must be an uninterrupted influx of new arrivals in glory. Imagine the literally millions of personal histories of God's grace in the lives of his children to be told and retold among heaven's residents. There was certainly much reason to glorify God for preserving dear Polly by his grace all the years of her life, to her very last day on earth.

Then there's the matter of her settling into her heavenly home, her "place." Jesus said that He would be "preparing a place" for us when He returned to heaven (John 14:2-3). What this entails we can only speculate. I love what C.S. Lewis said about this: "Your place in heaven will seem to be made for you and you alone, because you were made for it—made for it stitch by stitch as a glove is made for a hand."[79] *At home with the Lord* indeed (II Cor. 5:8).

Many times during our life we had travelled from home for various lengths of time. I remember the smile on Polly's face when we would pull up in front of our house and open the front door.

No matter how much we had enjoyed our trip (or not), we were so glad to be home. Home, sweet home. I can only imagine how much more "at home" she felt when she arrived at her heavenly destination.

How she is occupying her time in heaven I do not fully know, but I personally think there's enough evidence in Scripture for us to speculate that among other things, those in heaven may indeed be *praying* for those of us still on earth. The saints described in Rev. 6:9-10 are certainly praying for God's justice to be done on earth; and the *prayers of all the saints* are said to be symbolically offered through the incense in the heavenly temple (Rev. 8:3-4; 5:8). If they pray for us, could it be that they also are informed about us to some degree? I don't think it's beyond possibility that they are. The angels of God would certainly know many things about us, and new arrivals of people acquainted with our recent history would be able to inform our loved ones about our lives.[80] Moses and Elijah were aware of what was about to transpire in Jesus' life when they joined Him on the Mount of Transfiguration (Luke 9:30-31).

What we do know for sure is that those in heaven are overcome with the greatness and goodness of God, and are moved from the heart to praise and worship Him (Rev. 4-5). Lewis wrote about our worship in heaven: "Surely...each of the redeemed shall forever know and praise some one aspect of the divine beauty better than any other creature can. Why else were individuals created, but that God, loving all infinitely, should love each differently?... If all experienced God in the same way and returned Him an identical worship, the song of the Church triumphant would have no symphony, it would be like an orchestra in which all the instruments played the same note."[81] Skeptics complain that God must have a fragile ego if He demands to be worshiped by all his creatures, but they completely miss the point. The reality is that when we fully apprehend the greatness and goodness of God, worship will be the only possible response—for we will see how *worthy* He is to receive our heartfelt worship and praise (Rev. 4:11; 5:9, 12).

One thing for which He certainly will deserve praise is the marvelous *transformation* that will take place in each of us when we enter into glory. John says that *we will be like Him, because we will see Him just as He is* (I Jn. 3:2). All of us know people who have impacted and influenced us, changed us, just by being in their presence and enjoying their fellowship. If the presence of other mortals has this kind of effect on us, how much more must the presence of the immortal Son of God. Even now, we are told, as we behold the glory of the Lord we *are being transformed into the same image from glory to glory, just as from the Lord, the Spirit* (II Cor. 3:18). If our veiled vision of Christ changes us now, how much more when we see Him face to face? *Having no spot or wrinkle...but holy and blameless* before Him (Eph. 5:27). Our internal struggle with sin described so intensely in Romans chapter 7 will be forever a thing of the past.

Of course, as a result of this internal change, our *relationships* with others will be perfected as well. We often think of being reunited with loved ones in heaven. Who of us, however, has loved perfectly even our closest and dearest family and friends—not to mention brothers and sisters whom we may have injured, or by whom we were even deeply hurt during this life? We tend to romanticize our relationships, but this healing of relationships is a very real part of the spiritual transformation that will take place. I've wondered if in fact some of those who helped put Jesus to death might not be in heaven. Didn't He pray that the Father might forgive those who knew not what they were doing? In heaven, we'll be able to do the same. Jesus' prayer that we be *perfected in unity* will be finally and fully answered (Jn. 17:23).

Jonathan Edwards is most remembered for his sermons on hell, but he also wrote beautifully of heaven: "No inhabitants of that blessed world will ever be grieved with the thought that they are slighted by those that they love, or that their love is not fully and fondly returned.... There shall be no such thing as flattery or insincerity in heaven, but there perfect sincerity shall reign through all in all. Everyone will be just what he seems to be, and will really have all the love that he seems to have. It will not be as in this world, where comparatively few things are what they seem to be, and where professions are often made lightly and without meaning. But there, every expression of love shall come from the bottom of the heart, and all that is professed shall be really and truly felt."[82]

Our *knowledge* too will be greatly expanded. *For now we see in a mirror dimly, but then face to face; now I know in part, but then I will know fully just as I also have been fully known* (I Cor. 13:12). Not that our minds will ever encompass all that is in the infinite mind of God. Faith is one of the things that will abide forever (v. 13); and faith implies incomplete understanding. No doubt, however, many of the mysteries of this life will be resolved for us. I don't know if all our questions will be answered. I don't know if I will fully comprehend why Polly's earthly journey followed the

221

course it did. Yet I do believe that we will be satisfied that God's ways are ultimately just. How else could all our tears be dried, if this were not the case?

When I think of Polly in heaven, I think of Paul's words in Rom. 8:18 that *the sufferings of this present time are not worthy to be compared with the glory that is to be revealed to us.* These words were written by one who had endured great suffering in his life. Reading over the catalog of Paul's afflictions in II Corinthians 11:23-29 is a humbling experience. His sufferings were severe by any measure. In light of this fact, how great must be the glory that awaits us in heaven.

Isaiah tells us that in the new heaven and new earth, *the former things will not be remembered or come to mind* (Isa. 65:17). *The former things* he is referring to are the *troubles* of this life (v. 16). One day, the trials of this life—even those that may have lasted our entire lifetime—will be barely a glimmer of a memory. This is my great joy for Polly.

It is not, however, my greatest joy for her—for when we see the Lord in heaven, not only will our sorrows by consoled, but then the deepest and truest longings of our heart will be fulfilled. David said, *As for me, I shall behold Your face in righteousness; I will be **satisfied** with Your likeness when I awake* (Ps. 17:15). *In*

Your presence is fullness of joy; In Your right hand there are plea-sures forever (Ps. 16:11b). There is much joy in this life, but it is fleeting. Fullness of joy will never be known here — only there. The greatest blessings of this life are merely small "foretastes" of and pointers to the things to come which are *better by far* (Phil. 1:23). C. S. Lewis was right when he wrote: "There have been times when I think we do not desire heaven, but more often I find myself wondering whether, in our heart of hearts, we have ever desired anything else."[83] "If I find in myself a desire which no experience in this world can satisfy, the most probable explanation is that I was made for another world." [84]

D. A. Carson writes: "In fact, we begin to wonder if some pain and sorrow in this life is not used in God's providential hand to make us homesick for heaven, to detach us from this world, to prepare us for heaven, to draw our attention to himself and away from the world of merely physical things."[85] I believe this is true. I remember meeting once a man in the hospital who had been fighting cancer for two years. During our conversation, his wife said to me, "We're fighting the cancer, but we don't want to be so in love with this life and this world that we lose our hope of heaven." I found myself saying an "amen" in my heart to her words.

I believe Scripture tells us something more. It tells us that our present sorrows can actually be used by God to forge and deepen our experience of future glory. There are two passages that tell us this is so. The first is Romans 8:16-17: *The Spirit Himself testifies with our spirit that we are children of God, and if children, heirs also, heirs of God and fellow heirs with Christ, if indeed we suffer with Him so that we may also be glorified with Him.* The second passage is II Corinthians 4:17: *For momentary, light affliction is producing for us an eternal weight of glory far beyond all comparison....*

The full nature of the connection between present suffering and future glory may only become clear to us when we are with the Lord, but some of it should not be too difficult to comprehend. For one, there is a glory and joy that comes only to those who have faithfully persevered through difficulty to reach the treasured destination. We pay hard earned money to purchase tickets just to watch men and women athletes do this all the time. So, there will be a joy that awaits those who persevere faithfully to the end through the difficulties of this life. Paul spoke in these terms when he said near the end of his life, *I have fought the good fight, I have finished the course, I have kept the faith* (II Tim. 4:7).

Second, there is a glory that comes from having experienced God's preserving and sustaining grace in carrying us through life's hills and valleys that can only be realized as an outcome of such a life's journey. There will be a wonder at how God has demonstrated his power, mercy and wisdom in using life's most difficult afflictions to accomplish what is good, both *in* us and *through* us in the lives of others. Such wonder will express itself in unreserved worship before his heavenly throne.

Third, there will be a depth of fellowship between ourselves and our Savior that will emerge only as a result of having experienced something of the nature of his own earthly sufferings. We know this on a purely human level, through the comradery that is uniquely shared by fellow teammates or by members of a combat battalion. So, the depth and quality of our relationship with Christ will be influenced by the degree to which we have endured life's trials in the same spirit as did He. Paul spoke of this when he declared his longing to *know Him and the power of His resurrection and the fellowship of His sufferings* (Phil. 3:10). Not only this, but I am confident that the depth of our fellowship with those who came alongside us in our sufferings will also be experienced in heaven for eternity.

Most of all, our sufferings will have given us opportunity to demonstrate the supreme value of being known and loved by God, regardless of what sacrifices we might have been called on to endure in remaining faithful to Him and his calling. What eternal glory will return to God for all that He meant to us in our temporal sufferings.[86]

The very day after Polly's passing I read again in the devotional "Our Daily Bread" these words: "Human existence has been marked by tragedy, heartache, disappointment, and evil. It's comforting to know that the time is coming when sorrow and death will pass away, and God Himself will wipe all tears from our eyes. Then we will experience the truth that 'the former things have passed away' (Revelation 21:4).... Are you burdened today by some seemingly insurmountable problem? Are you lonely, heartbroken, and disappointed? If you are a child of God, dwell on this reassuring thought: 'The sufferings of this present time are not worthy to be compared with the glory which shall be revealed in us' (Romans 8:18). A brighter day is coming when words such as *sighing, death,* and *tears* will all be obsolete."[87]

I can't resist including this much beloved quote from the last page of the last volume of Lewis' *Narnia Tales*: "(T)he things that began to happen after that were so great and beautiful that I cannot write them. And for us this is the end of all the stories, and we can most truly say that they all lived happily ever after. But for them it was only the beginning of the real story. All their life in this world and all their adventures in Narnia had only been the cover and the title page; now at last they were beginning Chapter One of the Great Story, which no one on earth has read; which goes on forever; in which every chapter is better than the one before."[88]

During Polly's life God often turned our attention to heaven, especially on those days when we were tempted to be discouraged—and there were not a few. On those days especially I found myself asking the question, "What kind of life do I want to look back on when I get to the end of life's journey?" I believe that asking that question often helped us to seek to live each "today" in light of "that day."[89]

I once read the story of Florence Chadwick, who was the first woman to swim across the 21 mile channel between Catalina Island and Palos Verde on the California coast in 1952. She first attempted it on July 4 of that year. One writer described her attempt this way: "The weather that day was not auspicious—the ocean was ice cold, the fog was so thick that she could hardly see the support boats that followed her, and sharks prowled around her. Several times, her support crew used rifles to drive away the sharks. While Americans watched on television, she swam for hours. Her mother and her trainer, who were in one of the support boats, encouraged her to keep going. However, after 15 hours and 55 minutes, with only half a mile to go, she felt that she couldn't go on, and asked to be taken out of the water.... Brian Cavanaugh, in *A Fresh Packet of Sower's Seeds*, noted that she told a reporter, 'Look, I'm not excusing myself, but if I could have seen land I know I could have made it.' The fog had made her unable to see her goal, and it had felt to her like she was getting nowhere. Two months later she tried again. The fog was just as dense, but this time she made it. After 13 hours, 47 minutes, and 55 seconds, she reached the California shore, breaking a 27-year-old record by more than two hours and becoming the first woman ever to complete the swim."[90] She finished her course because she knew the shoreline was not far ahead—even though she couldn't see it.

During this lifetime we do *groan within ourselves* (Rom. 8:23), but we *groan in hope* (v. 20); and thus, with the Apostle Paul, speaking of our ultimate redemption, *with perseverance we wait eagerly for it* (Rom. 8:25).

Since Polly's passing I have often reminded myself that these things, for which we both longed and hoped for, are her present reality and possession; and it brings me great comfort. I can honestly say that the sorrow I felt when I first experienced her absence has been overshadowed by the joy that I know she is experiencing in the glorious presence of our Lord. As all who have loved ones who have gone on to glory can understand, I would never bring her back.

John describes the New Jerusalem in these words (Rev. 22:1-5): *Then he showed me a river of the water of life, clear as crystal, coming from the throne of God and of the Lamb, in the middle of its street. On either side of the river was the tree of life, bearing twelve kinds of fruit, yielding its fruit every month; and the leaves of the tree were for the healing of the nations. There will no longer be any curse; and the throne of God and of the Lamb will be in it, and His bond-servants will serve Him; they will see His face, and His name will be on their foreheads. And there will no longer be any night; and they will not have need of the light of a lamp nor the light of the sun, because the Lord God will illumine them; and they will reign forever and ever.*

Come, Lord Jesus. Come.

SOME CLOSING WORDS

T he story you have just read is true. Our story, however, is not *your* story—and we all do have one. The story of our life. Like ours, everyone's story contains a mixture of joy and pain. For some, there is more joy. For many, there is more pain.

The question we all face, however, is whether we will permit our story to merge into God's story. Whether the mixture of joy and pain in our life will draw us to God, or turn us away from Him.

If you are uncertain about God, as to whether He exists, or if He does, whether He can be trusted—I urge you to resolve your uncertainties sooner rather than later. If He is indeed there, and if our relationship with Him has consequences not only for this life but for the next, then there is no more urgent matter than that of our relationship with Him.

If someone were to ask me why I am a believing Christian, I would tell them two things. First, I've found the evidence for God, and for his Son, Jesus Christ, to be more than persuasive. I'm absolutely convinced based on the evidence that there is indeed a Creator God. Scientists have known for the better part of a century the evidence which confirms that the universe had a beginning. It has not always been here. Common sense tells us that anything that had a beginning must have had a cause. It couldn't have caused itself; and it couldn't have come into existence without a cause. Consequently, it must have been caused by Another; and this "Other" must be immensely powerful to bring the cosmos into existence from nothing.[91]

Furthermore, when we take a closer look at the universe we see that it gives evidence of having been intricately designed. Take the human eye for example. Our human vision is stereoscopic, three dimensional, full color, self-focusing, self-regulating for light, self-cleaning (note our tear ducts), and self-protected (note our eye brows, lashes, and eye lids). Our vision is as complex as any video camera and monitor, the design of which none of us would ever attribute to mere chance or random natural processes. Why would we conclude this about our eyesight, unless we were already biased on other grounds against the existence of an Intelligent Designer?[92] Though I don't claim to understand everything about God or his creation, I am fully convinced that He exists.

In addition, I'm fully convinced that Jesus Christ was who He claimed to be—the very Son of God. How can we account for the many predictions of the Hebrew prophets about the Jewish Messiah fulfilled in his life? That He would be born in Bethlehem (Micah 5:2). That He would come at the precise time foretold by the prophet Daniel (Daniel 9:24-27).[93] That He would die in a manner consistent with what would become known as crucifixion as administered by the Romans (Psalm 22:16-18; Isaiah 53). These are just a few of the many prophecies fulfilled in Jesus' life.

Above all, how can we explain his resurrection from the dead? His tomb was discovered vacant on the third day. Not even his adversaries denied this. Rather, they spread the rumor that his followers had stolen his body, because it was missing (Matthew 28:11-15). Over the next forty days He appeared to his followers in his transformed body on several occasions in a manner that can hardly be attributed to hallucination or vision (I Corinthians 15:5-8). Groups of people do not have the same hallucination simultaneously. Furthermore, his followers were so convinced of the reality of Jesus' resurrection that they willingly gave up their lives unto death for the sake of their testimony. People don't willingly give their lives for a cause they know is not true. For these and other reasons, I have no doubt that Jesus is the Lord.[94]

Beyond these facts, however, I must confess that our own experience of God's mercy and grace has been more than compelling—as has been the experience of many others. Though life is indelibly marked by suffering and mystery, I cannot explain the life I have been privileged to live, apart from the grace and mercy of God.

I urge you to take every step needed to remove whatever obstacles are standing in the way of placing your trust in Him and his Son Jesus. Jesus said, *For God so loved the world, that He gave His only begotten Son, that whoever believes in Him shall not perish, but have eternal life* (John 3:16). St. Augustine wrote in his Confessions: "(F)or thou hast made us for thyself and restless is our heart until it comes to rest in thee."[95] If you have never done so, and if the following prayer truly reflects the convictions of your heart, you can offer it to Him now.

God, I believe You are there. Though I do not understand everything about You, I believe You made me for relationship with Yourself. I acknowledge that my sin, my desire to run my own life in my own way, has broken our relationship; and I desire for it to be mended. I believe that You made this possible by giving your own Son Jesus as payment for my sin, in my place. I'm placing my faith and trust in Him as my Savior and Lord. On the basis of what He has done in my behalf, forgive me for my sin, and let me begin a new life with You today. Amen.[96]

If you already know Him, but you are facing struggles in life beyond your strength (and we all will), then my prayer is that our story will be a source of encouragement to you in life's journey. We live in a broken world; and sooner or later, life will reveal our own personal brokenness as well. Such a revelation, however, rather than being intended to destroy us, is intended to make absolutely clear our total need for God, and the grace and mercy He offers to us in his Son, Jesus Christ. My prayer is that you may find Him worthy of your trust.

Cast your burden upon the Lord, and He will sustain you; He will never allow the righteous to be shaken. Psalm 55:22.

Blessed be the Lord who daily bears our burden, the God who is our salvation. Psalm 68:19.

ABOUT THE AUTHOR

Rick Rood is a native of Seattle, WA (born 1949), and was raised in the San Francisco Bay Area. He is a graduate of Seattle Pacific University (BA in history) and Dallas Theological Seminary (ThM in Old Testament), where he also completed work toward a PhD in theology (ABD). He has been a hospital chaplain with Healthcare Chaplains Ministry Association since 1996 (www. hcmachaplains.org). He provides pastoral care to patients and families at both an acute care and a psychiatric hospital in the Dallas, TX area. He also occasionally goes overseas to conduct teaching missions for the training of indigenous Christian workers, often in partnership with ACTS International (www.actsinternational.net). He has served as a pastor and seminary instructor, as well as with the ministries of International Students, Inc., and Probe Ministries. Rick cared for his late wife Polly for many years until her home going, after a long illness, in 2003. They have two dear children, a son and daughter. Rick and his new wife Li Lin were married in Taipei, Taiwan, in 2012. They reside in the Dallas, TX area. Rick enjoys reading, walking, and hiking, but most of all his family.

ENDNOTES

1   The title of this chapter is taken from the book by Eugene H. Peterson, *A Long Obedience in the Same Direction: Discipleship in an Instant Society* (Downers Grove, IL: InterVarsity Press, 1980).

2   The phrase "Future Grace" is drawn from John Piper's book *Future Grace: The Purifying Power of the Promises of God* (Colorado Springs: Multnomah Press, 2012).

3   John R. W. Stott, *The Cross of Christ* (Downers Grove, IL: InterVarsity Press, 1986), 311.

4   For a clinical description of Huntington's Disease see the website of the Huntington's Disease Society of America: www.hdsa.org

5   This was a comment made to me by my friend Dr. David Wallace.

6   The analogy of trusting in a doctor or lawyer was first brought to my attention through the evangelistic booklet "How to have a happy and meaningful life" published by Dallas Theological Seminary (2005).

7   See the interview regarding testing for HD of Dr. Nancy Wexler on National Public Radio, May 16, 2004. http://www.npr.org/features/feature. php?wfld=1897199. Though some couples choose to take the genetic test in

determining whether or not to have children, the decision is a difficult one that has many ramifications for a person's life. Whether one should take this test is really a personal decision that should be made freely and voluntarily, in my opinion.

8   For insight into some of the challenges and dilemmas faced by persons at risk for Huntington's Disease, see the discussion in John S. and Paul D. Feinberg, *Ethics for a Brave New World*, 2nd Edition (Wheaton: Crossway, 2010), 464-76, 530ff. Their discussion is all the more relevant in light of the fact that John's wife has suffered with Huntington's Disease for many years.

9   Quoted in Dr. Archibald D. Hart, *Dark Clouds, Silver Linings* (Colorado Springs: Focus on the Family Publications, 1993), 161.

10   John R. W. Stott, *The Message of Thessalonians* (Downers Grove: InterVarsity Press, 1991), 126. Stott expands on these thoughts in his comments on Ephesians 5:20: "Although the text reads that we are to give thanks *always and for everything*, we must not press these words literally. For we cannot thank God for absolutely 'everything', including blatant evil. The strange notion is gaining popularity in some Christian circles that the major secret of Christian freedom and victory is unconditional praise; that a husband should praise God for his wife's adultery and a wife for her husband's drunkenness; and that even the most appalling calamities of life should become subjects for thanksgiving and praise. Such a suggestion is at best a dangerous half-truth, and at worst ludicrous, even blasphemous. Of course God's children learn not to argue with him in their suffering, but to trust him, and indeed to thank him for his loving providence by which he can turn even evil to good purposes (*e.g.* Rom. 8:28). But that is praising God for being God; it is not praising him for evil. To do this would be to react insensitively to people's pain (when Scripture tells us to weep with those who weep) and to condone and even encourage evil (when Scripture tells us to hate it and to resist the devil). God abominates

evil, and we cannot praise or thank him for what he abominates."
John R. W. Stott, *The Message of Ephesians* (Downers Grove:
InterVarsity Press, 1979), 207.

11 John Swinton, *Raging With Compassion: Pastoral Responses
to the Problem of Evil* (Grand Rapids: Wm. B. Eerdmans Publishing
Co., 2007), 113.

12 D. A. Carson, *The Gospel According to John* (Grand Rapids:
William B. Eerdmans Publishing Co., 2005), 362.

13 I owe this recollection to my former ISI colleague, Dan Brannen.

14 http://www.aging.ohio.gov/news/pressreleases/2011

15 John Swinton, *Dementia: Living in the Memories of God*
(Grand Rapids: Wm. B. Eerdmans Publishing Co., 2012), 280.

16 These were the words of my friend Rev. Grady Hinton, former
Director of Pastoral Care at Baylor Medical Center, Garland, TX.

17 I'm indebted to my training for hospital chaplaincy through
Healthcare Chaplains Ministry Association for my greater appreciation for the value of listening. These thoughts on the importance
of listening are gleaned from their excellent training curriculum.

18 One of the most helpful resources on listening, and ministering
to the suffering that I have found is the book by H. Norman Wright,
*Helping Those Who Hurt: How to Be There For Your Friends in
Need* (Minneapolis: Bethany House, 2003).

19 Quoted by Richard Payne, "Hope in the Face of Terminal Illness"
in *Living Well and Dying Faithfully*, edited by John Swinton and
Richard Payne (Grand Rapids: William B. Eerdmans Publishing
Company, 2009), 221.

20 Cf. H. Norman Wright, *Helping Those Who Hurt*, 77. I'm indebted to Norman Wright for this and many other insights on helping the suffering.

21 http://fallibleblogma.com/index.php/quote-of-the-day-small-things-with-great-love Accessed July 29, 2013.

22 Blaise Pascal, *Pensees* Tr. by A. J. Krailshaimer (London: Penguin Books, 1966), 316.

23 Among the many books written on Psalm 23, I found the book written by John J. Davis to be a special blessing: *The Perfect Shepherd: Studies in the Twenty-Third Psalm* (Grand Rapids: Baker Book House, 1980).

24 A. W. Tozer, *The Knowledge of the Holy* (New York, Evanston, London: Harper & Row Publishers, 1961), 9.

25 For the names of God, see Charles C. Ryrie, *Basic Theology* (Wheaton: Victor Books, 1987), 45-50.

26 I was first alerted to this passage by David Roper in his book *Psalm 23: The Song of a Passionate Heart: Hope & Rest from the Shepherd* (Grand Rapids: Discovery House Publishers, 1994), 32.

27 My memory fails me as to the source of these thoughts about the need of sheep for a shepherd.

28 Psalm 37:4 does tell us, *Delight yourself in the Lord; And He will give you the desires of your heart.* However, this surely does not mean that He will grant every request. (Cf. James 4:3.) In the words of Allen Ross: "(I)f the righteous delight in the LORD, then their petitions will be in harmony with his will." Allen P. Ross, *A Commentary on the Psalms: Volume I (1-41)* (Grand Rapids: Kregel Publications, 2011), 807.

29 Ibid., 561.

30 Ibid., 562.

31 Ibid., 571.

32 Ibid., 563.

33 Phillip Keller, *A Shepherd Looks at Psalm 23* (Minneapolis: World Wide Publications, 1970), 82.

34 F. B. Meyer writes of the significance of the change in pronouns in his book *The Shepherd Psalm* (Geanies House, Fearn, Ross-shire, Great Britain: Christian Focus Publications, 2005), 53.

35 Ross, *Psalms*, 1, 566.

36 Roper, *Psalm 23*, 117.

37 Cf. Isaiah 25:6.

38 Cf. Luke 15:4-7.

39 An excellent source for those caring for a loved one with Alzheimer's disease is *Alzheimer's: Caring for Your Loved One, Caring for Yourself*, by Sharon Fish (Wheaton: Harold Shaw Publishers, 1990).

40 "Christmas in Heaven" by Dr. Albert Simpson Reitz, www. thoughts-about-god.com/poems/christmas-heaven.html Accessed July 23, 2013.

41 The title of this chapter is taken from the book by Eugene H. Peterson, *A Long Obedience in the Same Direction: Discipleship in an Instant Society* (Downers Grove, IL: InterVarsity Press, 1980).

42 Jesus' comments to his disciples about the man born blind confirm the fact that not all sickness is due to personal sin (John 9:1-3).

43 The healing of the man at the pool of Bethesda is apparently a case where personal sin was at the root of illness. Jesus said to

him after his healing, *"Behold, you have become well; do not sin anymore, so that nothing worse happens to you"* (5:14).

44   John Wimber, "Signs, Wonders, & Cancer" in *Christianity Today*, October 7, 1996, p. 50.

45   One of the better books on divine healing in my opinion is Richard Mayhue's *The Healing Promise: Is it always God's will to heal?* (Geanies House, Fearn, Ross-shire, Great Britain: Christian Focus Publications, 2001).

46   Joni Eareckson Tada, *Heaven: Your Real Home* (Grand Rapids: Zondervan Publishing House, 1995).

47   These thoughts on vows in marriage were inspired by Mike Mason, *The Mystery of Marriage* (Portland, OR: Multnomah Press, 1984), 91-110.

48   My thinking in this chapter has been guided in large part by Frederick J. Gaiser's book, *Healing in the Bible: Theological Insight for Christian Ministry* (Grand Rapids: Baker Academic, 2010), particularly chapter 3.

49   I believe I owe this comparison to a statement by Robert D. Orr, M.D. in his book *Medical Ethics and the Faith Factor: A Handbook for Clergy and Health-Care Professionals* (Grand Rapids: William B. Eerdmans Publishing Co., 2009). I could not locate the exact place in this book where he makes a statement to the effect that to pray for healing without using appropriate medical resources is comparable to a farmer praying for a good harvest without plowing his field, sowing seed and watering his plants. The point is well taken.

50   R. K. Harrison, "Physician" *The International Standard Bible Encyclopedia: Fully Revised,* Four Volumes (Grand Rapids: William B. Eerdmans Publishing Co., 1979-1988), III, 865.

51 "Ecclesiasticus, or The Wisdom of Jeshua, The son of Sirach" 38: 1-14, in *The Apocrypha*, Tr. by Edgar J. Goodspeed (New York: Vintage Books, 1989), 295-96.

52 "Our Daily Bread" is available from RBC Ministries, P.O. Box 2222, Grand Rapids, MI 49501-2222.

53 "Say It Now!" by Richard De Haan, in "Our Daily Bread" July 24, 2003 (Grand Rapids: RBC Ministries, 2003).

54 For a collection of very helpful and insightful essays on end of life ethics and care (as well as other related topics) see John F. Kilner, Arlene B. Miller, Edmund D. Pellegrino (Eds.), *Dignity and Dying: A Christian Appraisal* (Grand Rapids: William B. Eerdmans Publishing Company, 1996).

55 "Unexpected Grief" by Dave Branon, in "Our Daily Bread" August 5, 2003 (Grand Rapids: RBC Ministries, 2003).

56 H. C. Leupold, *Exposition of The Psalms* (Grand Rapids: Baker Book House, 1969), 808.

57 "Gone From My Sight" by Henry Van Dyke. http//allpoetry. com/poem/9642757-Gone_From_My_Sight-by-Henry_Van_Dyke Accessed July 22, 2013.

58 I believe I owe this insight to D. A. Carson, though I could not find the exact reference in his book *How Long, O Lord? Reflections on Suffering and Evil,* Second Edition (Grand Rapids: Baker Academic, 2000).

59 I was first alerted to the fact that our lives bear witness to the angelic world by Joni Eareckson Tada, in her book *When God Weeps: Why Our Sufferings Matter to the Almighty* (Grand Rapids: Zondervan Publishing House, 1997), 107f.

60 I'm not sure where I first heard this statement; but I believe it was a statement made by Professor Norman L. Geisler in a class on apologetics at Dallas Theological Seminary.

61 John Goldingay, *Psalms: Volume 2, Psalms 42-89* (Grand Rapids: Baker Academic, 2007), 413.

62 Tada, *When God Weeps*, 84.

63 John Goldingay, *Songs From a Strange Land: Psalms 42-51* (Downers Grove, IL: InterVarsity Press, 1978), 35.

64 My memory fails me as to the original source of this idea.

65 Dorothy Sayers, *Letters to a Diminished Church* (Nashville: Thomas Nelson, 2004), 2.

66 Dr. John Kilner, *Life on the Line: Ethics, Aging, Ending Patients' Lives, And Allocating Vital Resources* (Grand Rapids: William B. Eerdmans Publishing Co., 1992), 104.

67 Paul Tournier, *Creative Suffering* (San Francisco: Harper & Row, 1983), 28.

68 My attention was drawn to some of these passages by the discussion of Justin S. and Lindsey A. Holcomb in their book, *Is It My Fault? Hope and Healing for Those Suffering Domestic Violence* (Chicago: Moody Publishers, 2014), chapter 10.

69 One of the better books I've read in recent times on the issue of suffering in the Christian's life is Timothy Keller's book, *Walking with God through Pain and Suffering* (New York: Dutton, 2013).

70 A very helpful resource on grief is H. Norman Wright's book *Recovering from the Losses of Life* (Grand Rapids: Fleming H. Revell, 1995). A small book of meditations was also helpful to me in the year after Polly's passing: *Grieving the Loss of Someone You Love: Daily Meditations to Help You through the Grieving*

Process, by Raymond R. Mitsch and Lynn Brookside (Ann Arbor, MI: Servant Publications, 1993).

71   J. I. Packer, *A Grief Sanctified: Passing Through Grief to Peace and Joy* (Ann Arbor, MI: Servant Publications, 1997), 12.

72   I cannot recall where I first read this exact description of Job's response.

73   I'm not sure where I first heard this statement; but it is true. My thoughts on the Ecclesiastes passage, however, were gleaned in part from the comments of Drs. Henry Cloud and John Townsend in their book *How People Grow: What the Bible Reveals About Personal Growth* (Grand Rapids: Zondervan, 2001), 228

74   A book that helped me understand how the grieving process can become a growth process was R. Scott Sullender's book *Grief and Growth: Pastoral Resources for Emotional and Spiritual Growth* (New York: Paulist Press, 1985). Sullender helped me realize that one of the functions of grief and loss is to teach us that no one can ultimately take the place of God in our life. God gives us many friends and loved ones in this life; but even if all of these should be taken from us, we still have the Lord—and in the final analysis, He is enough.

75   These were the words of my friend Dr. Willie Peterson.

76   "Unexpected Grief" by Dave Branon, in "Our Daily Bread" August 5, 2003 (Grand Rapids: RBC Ministries, 2003).

77   The phrase "Future Grace" is taken from John Piper's book, *Future Grace: The Purifying Power of the Promises of God* (Colorado Springs: Multnomah Books, 2012).

78   I once spoke with a gentleman who was a patient in the hospital I serve who told me that he had such an encounter. His family told me that he has never been the same since. His life was transformed.

79 C. S. Lewis, *The Problem of Pain* (New York: Macmillan, 1968), 147-48.

80 Herman Bavinck, *Reformed Dogmatics* (Four Volumes) Ed. by John Bolt. Tr. by John Vriend. (Grand Rapids: Baker Academic, 2003-2008), IV, 641.

81 Ibid., 150.

82 Jonathan Edwards, *Heaven: A World of Love* (Amityville, NY: Calvary Press, 1999), 27-29.

83 Lewis, *The Problem of Pain*, 145.

84 C. S. Lewis, *Mere Christianity* (New York: Macmillan, 1967), 120.

85 Carson, *How Long, O Lord*, 116.

86 These thoughts may give us some insight into how there can be degrees of reward for believers in heaven. Might it not be that our capacity for fellowship with the Lord (and with one another), as well as for genuine worship of the Lord, will be shaped in large measure by the degree to which we have faithfully walked with Him through the sufferings of this life, and experienced his transforming and sustaining grace? Millard J. Erickson has important words to say about this in his book *Christian Theology* (Grand Rapids: Baker Book House, 1985), 1233-34.

87 "Obsolete" by Richard De Haan, in "Our Daily Bread" August 7, 2003 (Grand Rapids: RBC Ministries, 2003).

88 C. S. Lewis, *The Last Battle* (New York: Collier Books, 1970), 183-84.

89 I first read this sentiment expressed in the writings of Martin Luther; but I cannot recall the exact reference.

90 From the *Gale Encyclopedia of Biography*, www.answers.com/topic/florence-chadwick Accessed May 26, 2014.

91 This argument for the existence of God is known as the "Cosmological Argument." For a more complete description of this argument see Paul Copan & William Lane Craig, *Creation out of Nothing: A Biblical, Philosophical, and Scientific Exploration* (Grand Rapids: Baker Academic, 2004).

92 This argument for God is known as the "Argument from Design" or the "Teleological Argument." For a discussion of this argument see William A. Dembski ed., *Mere Creation: Science, Faith & Intelligent Design* (Downers Grove, IL: InterVarsity Press, 1998).

93 For confirmation of this fact, see Harold W. Hoehner, *Chronological Aspects of the Life of Christ* (Grand Rapids: Zondervan Publishing House, 1977), Ch. VI. Hoehner convincingly demonstrates that Daniel's prophecy forecasts the coming of the Messiah on March 30, AD 33, the day of Jesus' "triumphal entry" into Jerusalem.

94 For a more complete discussion of the evidence that Jesus is the Son of God see Lee Strobel, *The Case for Christ: A Journalist's Personal Investigation of the Evidence for Jesus* (Grand Rapids: Zondervan Publishing House, 1998).

95 *The Confessions of St. Augustine*. Translated and edited by Albert Cook Outler (Mineola NY: Dover Publications, 2002), 1.

96 Elements of this prayer have been adapted from the prayer included in the booklet "How to have a happy and meaningful life", published by Dallas Theological Seminary. See note 2 above.

CPSIA information can be obtained at www.ICGtesting.com
Printed in the USA
LVOW08s2008210115

423790LV00002B/2/P